GIRL or BOY?

Your Chance to Choose

A clear and fascinating examination of all the theories and techniques which could help you to choose your baby's sex.

GIRL OR BOY?
Your Chance to Choose

by

Hazel Phillips
with
Tessa Hilton

Thorsons
An Imprint of HarperCollinsPublishers

Thorsons
An Imprint of HarperCollins*Publishers*
77–85 Fulham Palace Road,
Hammersmith, London W6 8JB

First published by Thorsons 1985

7 9 10 8

A catalogue record for this book
is available from the British Library

ISBN 0 7225 1131 0

Printed and bound in Great Britain by
Caledonian International Book Manufacturing Ltd, Glasgow

To my mixed family,
Sheena
Penny
Dick
and to my co-operative husband who made it possible.

HAZEL PHILLIPS

ACKNOWLEDGEMENTS

I am most grateful to my father, Sir Clement Chesterman OBE, MD, FRCP, for his constant interest and encouragement. Also to my girls for giving me the idea in the first place and for forgiving me for calling them mistakes, to my son for upholding the theory and being conceived on the day of ovulation and to my husband for doing it all right.

HAZEL PHILLIPS

Very many thanks to all the medical and biological scientists and doctors who were kind enough to help with information about their work and whose advice and comments were invaluable. And of course to the families — both those featured in this book and many more not mentioned — who put Hazel's method to the test and told us about their attempts to choose the sex of their baby.

TESSA HILTON

CONTENTS

10 GIRL OR BOY? Your chance to choose

INTRODUCTION

The secret of sex selection has proved Nature's hardest nut to crack. Scientists may be able to mix up life in a glass dish, but we still do not know enough to be sure of conceiving a boy or a girl baby.

As long as records have been kept, the ratio of men to women has always remained remarkably constant. Between 105 and 106 boys are born to every 100 girls but, because there is a slightly higher rate of miscarriage and infant death amongst boy babies, this evens out to an almost level fifty-fifty. Whatever the mechanism, it seems sophisticated enough to take account of factors which might upset the balance.

It might seem that we meddle with such a well-designed scheme at our peril, but there is no doubt that from time immemorial people have wanted to be able to choose the sex of their children — and that desire is no less present today.

Most obviously, it could be used to help families plagued by hereditary diseases like haemophilia, which can be carried by girls but only affects boys. It might act as a form of population control in some countries and, amongst nationalities where women are still second-class citizens whose worth is measured by their ability to produce sons, daughters would begin to be born only as wanted children and their status would rise accordingly. And all parents everywhere would have the privilege of being able to enjoy children of both sexes.

How close is science to finding an answer? In America there is a company which offers women a 70 per cent chance of having a son through artificial insemination. And important progress has been made in this country in animal research, where the knowledge that would enable cattle breeders to be sure of producing bulls or heifers would have obvious value. However, it will take many years before we know if these techniques can safely be used with humans, and the method could still only be used with artificial insemination.

Meanwhile there remain many parents of sons who would love a daughter, and parents of daughters who would like to try to tip the balance in favour of a son.

This book holds no absolute answers. It is an account of one woman, Hazel Phillips, who wanted a mixed family and thought a great deal about how to get one. She worked out a formula, followed it, and produced the son she wanted following two daughters. Since then, more than a hundred couples have also put her theory to the test with a success rate of 80 per cent.

Can Hazel's ideas really hold an answer? Tessa Hilton, a journalist, has looked critically at the basis of her theory, at the race between teams of biological and medical scientists to find the key to sex selection and at some of the issues which would be raised by the discovery of a guaranteed way of choosing the sex of your baby.

The result makes fascinating reading for anyone planning to have a baby as well as for those who are already parents.

1.

HAZEL'S STORY

Hazel Phillips didn't think very much about what you will later be reading when she first started her family. Indeed, she became pregnant by accident just two months after her marriage. But it was this accidental, and subsequently much-loved, baby which started her quest to discover the secret of sex selection. And it must be the same spirit which refuses to accept limitations in her own personal life, which also makes her refuse to be daunted in the face of a question which has baffled the scientific world for centuries.

Hazel suffers from multiple sclerosis: an incurable and progressive disease which first manifested itself when she was sixteen years old and playing in a school tennis match. 'I just suddenly began to miss the ball,' recalls Hazel. 'My limbs simply wouldn't do as I was telling them.'

Her father, a doctor who was later knighted for his services to medicine, immediately diagnosed what he had suspected for some time. But, out of a spirit of protectiveness, he did not tell his daughter. And, although problems of various kinds continued to affect her eyes and movement, it was another ten years before Hazel herself had any idea what was wrong. It fell to a medical student at the Middlesex Hospital to break the news.

'I was expecting my third baby and sitting with the other pregnant mums at the antenatal clinic,' says Hazel. 'We were all waiting to see the doctor when this student put his head round the cubicle curtains and called out: "Who's the patient with multiple sclerosis?"

'We all looked round to see who would come forward and no one did, so he called again. I suddenly thought "I wonder if he means me?" I got up and went to see and there it was written on my notes.'

The fact that she had been married and gone through two pregnancies without bothering to inquire if her illness had a name speaks volumes about Hazel's refusal to dwell on her own problems, about her continuing interest in other people and ideas and about her ability totally to dismiss her difficulties as being anything more than a slight bore.

'Of course I knew there was something wrong with me but I didn't know it had a specific label,' she says. 'Remember, in those days no one knew much about MS — there certainly weren't articles in magazines as there are today. And, in fact, although it might sound a harsh way to find out I shall always be grateful to that medical student, because then I knew what I had to cope with.'

And although what she had to cope with prevented her from going to university, she trained as a teacher instead and it was while at college that she met her husband, Nigel, now a University lecturer in Indonesian language and literature. They married when Hazel was twenty-one and, coming from a large and happy family — she was the youngest of three boys and two girls, she was keen to have children herself.

The only advice from her specialist was that if she must, then it had better be sooner rather than later. But daughter Sheena, born less than a year after they married, was rather sooner than even Hazel bargained for!

'My daughter Sheena was conceived on 19 November 1957 — I know the exact date because she was an accident, though a very successful one as it turned out!

'We mistakenly thought we were in the "safe period" because it was only the fifth day of my cycle, as soon as I had finished menstruating, and we didn't use any contraception that one time. The result — a lovely baby girl.'

Two years later the couple decided they wanted to enlarge

their family and try for another baby.

'As I seemed to be pretty fertile on the fifth day of my cycle, and that seemed to be when we could produce babies, we decided to repeat the procedure,' explains Hazel.

Sure enough she conceived immediately, again on the fifth day. But despite all Hazel's praying and willing for the opposite, they got another girl! This time daughter Penny, who Hazel describes affectionately as, 'Another mistake who has given us pleasure ever since!'

After this Hazel began to give the whole question some serious thought. She wanted a mixed family and felt sure that conceiving on the same day of her cycle twice and producing two daughters must be related facts.

'I have to admit that I was working on a completely unscientific hunch,' says Hazel. 'But the more I thought about it, the more I became convinced that sex determination must be linked with the day in the menstrual cycle that conception took place.

'At the back of my mind I felt that, since women are generally more long lived and tenacious in life, the same rule might apply to the female-producing sperm at conception. So that in a race on the peak day of ovulation the males would win, but over a period of days the more enduring females would survive better while waiting for the egg.'

So Hazel decided that, in the hope of conceiving a boy the third time, they would reverse the procedure and, instead of trying early in the cycle, aim for conception on the day of ovulation.

'I set about determining my day of ovulation, and every day for six months I took my temperature before getting out of bed and kept a record of the readings.

'I was lucky because, as soon as I began to be more aware of my fertile period, I realized that around the time of ovulation I always had a slight, jelly-like discharge from the vagina, like the white of an egg.

'This helped me to plot my chart and determine my exact

cycle, which was 24 days from the beginning of one period to the beginning of the next. I was able to pinpoint ovulation as the tenth day after starting a period.

'Having established this beyond doubt, we thought about our next child. Because no barrier methods of contraception can be totally effective, and because I wanted to give my theory every chance in the hope of getting a boy, we abstained from sex until the tenth day of my cycle — the day of ovulation. I conceived first time and I felt so sick for the next three months that I never doubted the outcome — a boy!'

So Hazel got her mixed family — Sheena, Penny and Dick who have since gone on to do her proud by each winning scholarships to either Cambridge or Oxford. But of course, for the next few years she was kept more than busy bringing them up. So it wasn't until they were grown up that she was able to pursue her theory of sex selection in the form of a little booklet which she published herself several years ago.

By this time she had read as much as she could find on the subject and was delighted to discover that many doctors around the world agreed with her theories, although she had arrived at them quite independently. In particular an American gynaecologist, Landrum B. Shettles, thought that timing held the secret, and we shall look at his work in more detail later.

Hazel's booklet was written about in *Mother and Baby* magazine, which invited readers who wanted a particular sex to act as guinea-pigs and put Hazel's theories to the test. The Family Planning Association, who get regular requests for information on the subject, also photocopied the article, and then there were the friends of friends who heard about it and so requests began to filter in for copies of the booklet.

But what was even more interesting was, about a year later, when the results of couples who tried the method began to come back. It turned out that what had worked for Hazel was working for slightly over 80 per cent of other families too.

And today a visit to the Phillips' home is evidence of the increasing response to Hazel's ideas. Although now quite severely restricted in her movements, phones in every room enable her to deal with the continual stream of calls she gets from women all over the world. And to hear Hazel talk makes it sound like a huge club. Mums ring her for advice, for a chat or to tell her the good news about the birth. And she remembers them . . . and their babies.

But it is typical of this remarkable woman that this is only part of her work. If you wander into the front of the house or gaze through to the pretty garden there are the paint pots and the bricks, the slides and the swings to tell you that, amazingly, three mornings a week this house is a riot of under fives. Together with two helpers Hazel has run her own hugely successful nursery school for the last eighteen years.

And, as if that's not enough, Hazel has just graduated from the Open University with a degree in science and philosophy.

It's not surprising that someone with such an inquiring mind and a zest for life should have wanted to unravel Nature's closest guarded secret!

2.

GIRL *OR* BOY —
MAKE SURE IT'S A
SUPERBABY!

So you're thinking about having a baby — did you know that this is exactly the right time to start caring about your future child's health? And if that sounds like an advert for health insurance — well, in a way, it is. Because what you put into looking after yourself now, before you actually conceive, can show as a head start in health for your baby when it's born.

Most women know that it is important to eat sensibly and take care of themselves during pregnancy. But there is increasing evidence that the state of our bodies at the time of conception and in the vital first few weeks of the baby's life (before you even know you are pregnant) matters even more.

And it's not just the difference between a handicapped and a normal baby. Because, even amongst babies born without defects, there is a wide range of conditions. Very small babies — described as low birth-weight babies — are far more at risk than their larger brothers and sisters. They are more likely to develop slowly and it is not known how long this poorer start in life continues to affect their growth.

And just as the physical conditions of normal babies can vary, so can their mental ability. A poor start in life, from the moment of conception, can make it harder for a baby to realize the full potential of its inherited intelligence quota.

What all parents care about, far more than having a boy or a girl, is having a healthy baby. If you are prepared to think about trying something which could give you a girl or a boy, doesn't it make sense to invest some thought now to make sure that, whatever its sex, yours is a real superbaby?

There are seven simple steps you can take, before you try to conceive, to help you have a superbaby with a head start on health for life:

1. *Rubella Check.* If you catch Rubella (or German Measles as it is more commonly known) in the first three months of pregnancy, it could leave your baby blind, deaf and mentally retarded. Ask your doctor to arrange a simple blood test to show if you are immune. If not, you can be vaccinated but you must not become pregnant within the three months following the vaccination. Even though the test and the vaccine are so simple, hundreds of babies each year are still damaged by German Measles.

2. *Contraception.* There is no suggestion that being on the Pill means a higher risk to future babies, but hormones play a critical part in the complex process of fertilization and it takes time for the effects of the Pill to work their way out of your system. Recommendations for the length of time you should stay off the Pill before trying to conceive vary between three and six months; in the meantime use a barrier method like the cap or sheath. Remember, you can't chart your temperature while on the Pill, either, because it affects ovulation.

Some hard-line pre-pregnancy experts also say women fitted with copper IUDs should have these taken out three months ahead of conception and use a barrier form of contraception, because the levels of copper in your body may be raised.

3. *Drugs.* Hard-learned lessons like the Thalidomide disaster have made us very aware of the dangers of drugs to the unborn baby — the same advice is just as true before and at the time of conception. If you have to take some form of long-term medication then talk to your doctor about it and, if you do get ill and need drugs, always tell your doctor if there is any chance you could be pregnant. Naturally, if you are unwell don't choose

that as a time to try for a baby — you probably won't feel like it anyway! The same advice obviously applies to illegal as well as legal varieties of drugs and, if you are reliant on some kind of drug and have become pregnant, tell your doctor and get advice and help from a specialist clinic. Avoid over-the-counter medicines as much as possible but don't get so hung up that you put up with a blinding headache all day rather than take an aspirin. Again, though, if you regularly have to take pain-killers you should seek advice.

4. *Smoking.*   There's no question about the advice on smoking and pregnancy — just *don't.* This applies just as much before conception, because the effects stay in your system for some weeks, depending on how heavily you smoke. Smoking definitely produces smaller babies and also makes the baby more at risk in the womb because it cuts the amount of oxygen supplied through the placenta. Mothers who smoke are also more likely to have threatened or actual miscarriages, and to have premature babies. It's just as important for your man to give up the dreaded weed too — tell him smoking is actually making him less fertile because it affects the motility and numbers of his sperm. Also, sitting in a smoky atmosphere can be just as bad as having a few cigarettes yourself, so there's no point in you struggling to resist a cigarette if he's puffing away like a bonfire — and that includes pipe-smoking, too. Finally, it's just plain unreasonable, if you both want a healthy baby, for him to expect you to give up alone. Nicotine is highly addictive and weaning yourself off needs will-power and help. It will be much easier for you to try giving up together.

5. *Drinking.*   It used to be thought that only really heavy drinking could affect babies — unfortunately, we now know differently. Women who drink even moderately before and around the time of conception and in the early weeks run a higher risk of miscarriage, or reducing the baby's birth-weight.
   Researchers at London's Charing Cross Hospital who looked

at the drinking habits of 900 women and the birth-weight of their babies suggested that women should cut their consumption to less than 100g of alcohol a week before pregnancy — that's about two glasses of wine — and of course it's better still to stop drinking altogether. (If you can't completely kick the wine habit then try diluting your white wine with some kind of fizzy water — it's a recognized drink called a spritzer for those who like to know what they're ordering — and drink it with a meal.) Again, the Charing Cross researchers made the point that these low birth-weight babies could continue to be disadvantaged in later life. One study of babies whose mothers were only moderate drinkers showed that at eight months these babies were still smaller and hadn't developed as fast mentally or physically as the same age group of babies with teetotal mothers. And there are good reasons for your man to cut down too — first, it's going to be good for his health in general and, second, it's his baby too and you need support, not just a chance to play the sober chauffeur! But drinking also does terrible things to sperms — one consultant estimated that if a man with a sperm count which was just adequate drank three to four pints a day this could reduce his sperm count to infertile levels. So, presumably, the more your man drinks over this limit, the higher his natural sperm count needs to be to withstand the ravages! However, a few weeks off the booze should be enough for him to recover his fertility.

6. *Diet.*   The diet you eat before you become pregnant should be not just good, but made up of the very best possible food. At the time of conception and during those first fragile weeks of life your body should contain the full quota of vitamins and trace elements which, according to ever-increasing evidence, are all-important factors in the early stages of development. We still don't know all the actions of these nutrients but they often have complex interlocking reactions — thus, a deficiency of one vitamin or mineral can prevent others from doing their

job properly. It has long been known that an iron deficiency results in anaemia and that pregnant women need more iron than usual. Zinc, too, is being considered of importance, and it is likely that the right balance of all the other trace elements may eventually be understood to be just as significant. Clinical trials are still going on, but studies suggest a link between babies born with neural tube defects, like spina bifida, and a deficiency of vitamins, folic acid in particular. Certainly it is known that pregnant women need more folic acid and that most deficiencies occur around January to March, probably because there are fewer fresh vegetables around. And, though animal studies can't be translated directly into human terms, a diet without folic acid causes all kinds of abnormalities in most animals. Other animal tests show that a diet without vitamin A in early pregnancy can lead to blindness, cleft palate and cleft lip, and a shortage of manganese can cause a deformity of the inner ear.

How, then, can you make sure your diet is bursting with all the goodness you need? Well, there is no need to spend a fortune on vitamin and mineral supplements because, in some cases, too much can be as potentially harmful as too little. It is much better to get all the nutrients you need from eating well. Then you are taking in your requirements in the most natural way possible, with little chance of exceeding safe limits. There are many good books around which spell out the details of healthy eating, but these are the basic rules to follow:

(a)   Look critically at what you already eat. It is a good idea to keep a record of your current diet over the course of ten days. It should be excellent, not just 'good enough'. The dietitian at your local antenatal clinic will probably be happy to advise you on its nutritional content, or check with a doctor specializing in pre-conceptual care — the address of the organization concerned with this subject is at the end of the book.

(b)   Cut out pre-packaged convenience foods wherever

possible and substitute fresh food. Don't be put off, thinking this has to mean endless preparing and cooking. Fresh fruit and a wholemeal cheese sandwich is far better for you than most instant tinned or frozen meals, and it's usually cheaper too!

(c)   Eat wholemeal bread and wholegrain products rather than white bread and foods made with white flour. Extend this to pasta, rice and cereals, and start reading labels — porridge, *Shredded Wheat* or *Weetabix* are wholegrain cereals, for example, while cornflakes and *Rice Krispies* are not.

(d)   Eat green leaf vegetables every day for folic acid, plus as much fresh fruit and raw vegetables as possible. When you do have to cook them, steam, microwave or boil them very lightly in a little water.

(e)   Vary red meat with poultry, fish, cheese, eggs, nuts and pulses — all good sources of protein.

(f)   Cut down on sweets, bought cakes, biscuits and puddings, fizzy drinks and instant packet mixes. They won't do you any good and often have lots of chemical additives.

(g)   There's no proof that coffee or saccharin are harmful, but some doctors think it's better to avoid them on the basis that you should give the baby the benefit of the doubt so don't use saccharin instead of sugar, and limit coffee drinking.

7. *Slimming.*   Just don't — following a slimming diet means not eating a balanced diet and missing out on many of the nutrients we've been talking about. More than that, a woman's fertility is reduced as she gets thinner until she reaches a weight at which she actually becomes infertile, and that point can be long before someone begins to look painfully thin. It has been found that some women become infertile at weights we used

to think ideal, and the Health Education Council has raised its recommended weights for women by 20 per cent. Studies show that babies born to women who were underweight before pregnancy are more at risk. It's a pity that Princess Diana set a fashion for the super-slim look during her second pregnancy. While it might be all right for a Princess, with the best possible care and supervision at every step, to sail close to the wind in the weighting game, it's not really an example to be copied. And even Princess Diana, with good health and youth on her side as well as privilege, still ended up with a baby weighing less than her first son. Better to give the baby the benefit of the doubt and leave the skinny look for post-pregnancy days. Of course, that doesn't mean we have to go back to the days of 'eating for two', and fertility can also be impaired by obesity, but if you eat a healthy diet without too much sugar or refined products, your weight should settle naturally at a healthy level.

3.

THE BIOLOGICAL BACKGROUND: A BEGINNER'S GUIDE TO X AND Y

Television documentaries seem to be full of guided tours round the human body these days — trips down undulating, frondy tunnels and past gently heaving hard-to-identify organs. It's all fairly mind-boggling, and they never do quite explain how they got the microscopic camera down there in the first place. With film around which has charted the long journey of the sperm through the womb to its eventual meeting and merging with the egg in the Fallopian tube, a mere peep down a microscope seems a bit old hat these days.

But for those who not only dozed through biology classes but have since steadfastly refused to read any of the hundreds of features about test-tube babies, a bit of basic know-how about the beginnings of life is essential to appreciate the whole question of how to try and tip the balance in favour of conceiving boys or girls.

A baby girl arrives in this world already kitted out for reproduction — all the eggs she will produce are already present in her ovaries in the form of primitive cells which will develop later. When a woman has an unborn baby girl inside her it's a bit like the Russian dolls — the egg which will make another person is inside the baby which is inside the mother!

The ovaries are pinkish-grey and about the size and shape of almonds — they lie one each side of the womb. Running from the top of the womb to the two ovaries are the Fallopian tubes. These are not actually joined to the ovaries but open instead into a trumpet shape which loosely cups around one end of each ovary. From puberty onwards, a complex series of hormone signals and reactions stimulate little round masses of cells, called follicles, inside the ovary to enlarge, making a fluid-filled sac with a ripening egg, or ovum, in the middle. Usually one egg is produced from alternate ovaries every month until the menopause. The follicle with an egg inside swells up until it finally appears as a bulge on the side of the ovary. When the egg breaks free, usually around the fourteenth day of the cycle, that is called ovulation.

The so-called test-tube baby technique involves collecting the egg before it passes out of the follicle. This is done using a long thin needle and a laparoscope — a long optical instrument which is inserted through a tiny cut and enables the surgeon to see the ovary and Fallopian tube. Until now it has been usual to give a fertility drug to women trying for a test-tube baby. This stimulates the ovary to produce several eggs at a time — up to 15 have been collected in one session.

In vitro fertilization (IVF) just means fertilization in glass — not, in fact, the famous test-tube but usually a flat laboratory bowl called a petri dish. Sperm and eggs are mixed together in the right kind of solution at the right temperature and, with any luck, more than one embryo results. An embryo can then be put back into the womb and the spares frozen to be used for subsequent attempts if the first is rejected. An amazing technological achievement, but our growing expertise with eggs, sperms and embryos has given rise to many ethical conundrums — we'll look at these in a later chapter.

To return to the story of life as it begins for eggs not 'hijacked' before ovulation: these break free from the ovary and fall into the arms of tiny frondy filaments around the entrance to the Fallopian tube. The waving motion of these fronds draws the egg into the tube, which has a diameter only about the width of a hairbrush bristle and is about four inches (10cm) long. The egg itself is somewhat smaller than the full stop at the end of this sentence.

This may seem small, but it's much larger than the sperm

— *twenty-five million* sperm would be needed to cover a full stop! This difference in size is because, while the sperm is the trigger for growth and contains all the genetic inheritance from the father, the egg has to contain all the programming needed to produce an embryo and its accompanying machinery. It also contains enough yolk to feed the embryo for a limited time until another source of food is established.

Sperms are the male reproductive cells and, as most people know, look like tiny wriggling tadpoles when viewed down a microscope. They are made in the testes, the two glands inside the scrotum, which have a tough, fibrous skin and coils of tubes inside which are produced the sperm. From puberty onwards millions of sperms are made — not just when a man has sex, but all the time. They have a short life outside the body — usually thought to be only 48 hours though live sperm have been found in women up to 72 hours after intercourse. We don't know if the sperm would still be able to fertilize the egg by this time.

Although only one sperm can fertilize the egg, each ejaculation can contain several hundred million. Unused sperms are reabsorbed back into the body, a process which still happens normally in men who have had vasectomies (a process of blocking or severing the tube leading from the testes).

Sperms move along by lashing their tails — it takes them roughly an hour of vigorous tail lashing to complete the seven inch (18cm) marathon from the cervix (neck of the womb) to the Fallopian tube where a ripe egg may or may not be waiting. The egg has no means of propulsion and has to rely on the rhythmic contractions of the tube to waft it along towards the womb.

Although the egg lives longer than the sperm (about five days) there are various changes in the egg which make it much easier for the sperm to penetrate 48 hours after ovulation. Scientists doing IVF work found eggs fertilized immediately after being plucked from the ovary often didn't develop and they now incubate them for several hours first.

In the days approaching ovulation, and during the fertile period, changes also take place in the mucus around the cervix and in the cervix itself which make it much easier for sperms to get through — outside the fertile period this mucus is impassable to sperm.

So you can see that the timing of conception is already quite a critical matter. But to understand more about science's attempts to pre-select males or females you need to get to the very heart of the matter — to what is inside the eggs and the sperm.

The nucleus is the information and control centre of every cell, and contains the chromosomes. These consist of two strands of the nucleic acid DNA (deoxyribonucleic acid, for the scientifically minded) which are coiled like a spring. In ordinary body cells we all have forty-six chromosomes arranged in twenty-three pairs. Twenty-two of the pairs are the same, but the twenty-third pair is the sex chromosomes which determine gender — in women this pair can only be a matching XX but in men this pair is made up of two different chromosomes, an X and a Y.

Just before a cell divides these pairs of chromosomes can be seen quite clearly arranged in their pairs. This pattern of the chromosomes is called a karyotype — a genetic blueprint of that person. But what can't be seen through a microscope, because they are so tiny, are the genes. These are the little chemical packages of instructions which contain all the information for the formation of a new person. They are arranged along the chromosomes and each cell contains about two million genes.

Eggs and sperms have a nucleus just like ordinary body cells — it is in the centre of the egg and in the head of the sperm. But a process called meiosis dictates that eggs and sperms only have half sets of chromosomes — 23 single chromosomes instead of 46 arranged in pairs.

During meiosis in men the full double set of chromosomes splits to make one single set with an X chromosome and one single set with a Y chromosome so sperms are either X- or Y-carrying. But, because women have a matching XX pair, meiosis can *only* produce half sets with an X, so all eggs are X-carrying.

After the sperm penetrates the egg these two half sets of chromosomes come together at fertilization to form a complete set of 46 chromosomes arranged in pairs — the beginning of a new life.

If a Y-carrying sperm fertilizes the egg then the XY combination means the baby will be a boy and if an X-carrying sperm gets there first the XX combination will become a girl.

Chromosome Tests to Determine Sex

Looking at the karyotype, or print-out, of an unborn baby's chromosomes can tell doctors if there is a major abnormality — the commonest example is Down's Syndrome which is shown by an extra chromosome. Other defects might show as damaged, chipped or missing chromosomes. And of course, in doing these tests, doctors can also see what sex the baby is, although many parents want to leave that as a surprise until the birth.

The commonest method of obtaining the material for these tests is still amniocentesis — a long, hollow needle is inserted through the abdomen to draw off some of the amniotic fluid in which the baby is floating. Some of the baby's cells, which are found in the fluid, can be cultured and then examined under a microscope. It is important to realize that there is a slight risk of miscarriage with the test (about one in a hundred) and it cannot be done before the sixteenth week of pregnancy. Growing and examining the cells and preparing a karyotype takes another three weeks, so if a couple decide they want to terminate the pregnancy because the baby is damaged the woman faces an abortion at possibly twenty weeks or even later — a physically distressing and emotionally traumatic experience.

A newer test to be perfected can be done between the sixth

and tenth week of pregnancy and gives results in hours, but may have higher risks. It is called chorionic biopsy and involves drawing off cells from inside the womb — again with a fine needle but this time through the cervix, which is easier. The cells are taken from the chorionic villi, which are protrusions from the wall of the womb which support the foetus in the early weeks and are then either incorporated as part of the placenta or disintegrate.

A new method of sexing embryos, which has been tried successfully with mice, is to use DNA probes which home in on the male or female chromosome. If this could ever be used with humans the sex of the child would be known shortly after the egg had been fertilized. It's also possible to sex embryos fertilized in the lab — the test-tube babies — though officially this hasn't been done with human embryos yet. Again, it means taking a sample of cells, but it is a tricky business to take the right ones and leave the embryo undamaged while it is still so small.

The only non-invasive technique of sex determination which does not involve the chromosomes at all is scanning — real experts claim to be able to tell the sex of a baby this way from as early as sixteen weeks but, generally, this is only a sure way of determining the sex later in the pregnancy and depends on the type of scanning machine and the experience of the person interpreting the picture.

4.

WHAT ELSE CAN SCIENCE TELL US?

People have never been short of an idea or two when it comes to the difficult question of how to choose the sex of a baby. Tying off one testicle was a favourite with the ancient Greeks — they believed that sperm from the left side meant girls and from the right, boys. Later French noblemen went one better and actually had the left testicle cut off in an attempt to produce an heir.

Sounds a touch too brutal? Then how about a spot of gentle gender bending as practised in the Palau Islands of the Pacific? Not much to it really, ladies, you just get your mate's clothes off, then put them on yourself. Might be a good idea to warn him about this routine in advance though!

Dressing up not your line either? Well, as you fling your inhibitions and clothes to the wind at least make sure you notice where your old man's Y-fronts end up — left side of the bed again for girls and right for boys.

Or you could be very cool about all this and let someone else do the work for you. Giving birth to a daughter in Austria could be followed by the midwife making a speedy exit from the delivery room clutching a kidney dish. Don't worry, she's just off to bury the placenta under the nearest nut tree to ensure you get a son next time around.

Sounds crazy? Well don't forget that even schemes like these can be guaranteed to work — at least half the time. Because the equally balanced ratio of boys to girls means we're members of the fifty-fifty club — whatever you do or don't do you still have a 50 per cent chance of getting the sex you want anyway.

But what can science tell us about the whole question? Over the years there have been literally hundreds of research papers published on the subject — lots of them contradict each other and many of them have caused an initial stir of interest only to be criticized later because they were based on unreliable information or there were flaws in the way the experiments or studies were conducted.

It could be that many factors conspire to keep the ratio of men and women equal. That in everything, from the changing hormone levels during a woman's cycle to the microchemical world we now know exists within the follicle of the ovary, from the condition and performance of the sperm to their internal DNA code combination, there is a series of complex checks and balances which work to ensure the numbers of males and females are kept equal. Or maybe there is even one over-riding mechanism which could be switched on and off to ensure the survival of the species in the face of threatened disaster?

Not all species have an equal number of males and females. Alligators, who could be said to be threatened, have a ratio of about six females to every male. In their case the sex ratio mechanism is simply heat — a warmer nest means more females. But don't all rush to turn the central heating up if you're hoping for a girl. Nowhere is there more variation amongst species than in the details of how they reproduce. Just because sea worms go a bundle on a potassium solution for producing males and a magnesium solution for females (which was the basis of a diet theory) it doesn't mean to say you can apply it to man.

Certainly, though, the scientists' failure to find an answer to the puzzle of sex pre-selection is not for want of looking. There are obvious financial rewards to be had in farming if someone could guarantee to produce cows or bulls by artificial insemination, and there is probably no less money to be made from being able to offer the same choice to parents.

So research continues, by zoologists, biologists, and

geneticists — often as a side issue to their main work, for example immunology.

These are some of the areas at which they have looked:

- Separating X and Y sperm in the laboratory to use for artificial insemination.
- Immunizing women against Y-carrying sperm.
- Changing conditions in the woman's reproductive system to favour one type of sperm at the expense of the other.
- The timing of intercourse in relation to the day of ovulation.

An allied area of research, which was mentioned earlier, is how to tell what sex the unborn baby is — preferably as early as possible in the pregnancy. There has been quite a lot of success here but unfortunately this could only be used as a method of sex selection if babies of the 'wrong' sex were then aborted, so it is unlikely ever to be used for this purpose, on ethical grounds.

But central to all the research has been the crucial question of how to tell the Y sperm from the X sperm — what are their differences? As far as the outside membranes of the sperm are concerned these differences are either very small and insignificant or non-existent. And, logically, since the sperm is only a delivery system to transport the important material inside, why should it need to be different on the outside?

So far, only one difference between the X and Y sperm seems undisputed — the X (girl-producing) chromosome is twice as large as the Y chromosome. But this is not the same as saying that the X-carrying sperm are twice as large as the Y-carrying sperm. Don't forget we are only talking about a difference in one chromosome and all the other 22 in each type of sperm are exactly the same. The result is just a slight difference in the amount of DNA — the X sperm have about 3 per cent more.

In theory, because of this slight difference in the amount of DNA, the X sperms should be heavier but, in practice, this small difference can be far outweighed by the overall weight of the sperm and its individual swimming ability. And sperm are not all the same size — although the amount of DNA inside might be different there can still be large Y sperm and small X sperm.

We mentioned before the work of the American gynaecologist Landrum B. Shettles and it was he who first popularized the idea of the slow-swimming, longer-living X (girl-producing) sperm and the faster-swimming, short-lived Y sperm in his book *Your Baby's Sex* (Bantam Books, 1980).

He also maintained that the pH factor made a difference to the sperms. This is a measure of the degree of acidity or alkalinity — so pH1 is pure acid and pH14 pure alkali. Dr Shettles recommended using douches of vinegar or bicarbonate of soda to get the balance right and said that the woman should also have an orgasm to increase the alkalinity of the vagina if she wanted a boy.

Shettles 'raced' the sperm through a filter soaked in cervical mucus and, using a test we'll describe later but which is difficult and gives very variable results, found the first few hundred sperm to pass through the filter were Y-bearing. But other scientists disputed the claims and further tests failed to find any differences in the length of time they lived, their size or any other outwardly detectable differences. The pH factor is important to the survival of both types of sperm and if the level is wrong then both X and Y are killed. But experiments have failed to show that different pH levels favour one type of sperm over another. That isn't to say that a difference doesn't exist but it suggests that if pH levels do matter, then the difference is very slight. It has been suggested that the pH factor may be the reason that slightly more boys are born than girls but, again, this is only a theory.

However, the theory of difference in weight and 'swimming' ability hasn't been resolved yet. A research biologist called Ronald Ericsson has revived this theory with a technique which he says can produce sperm for artificial insemination which is 80 per cent Y-bearing instead of the usual 50 per cent.

Working with other scientists he conducted an experiment

where a sample of sperm was put at the top of a glass column containing a solution of a protein found in blood. This solution had roughly the same consistency as semen and Ericsson found that it was thick enough to slow down the poorly swimming sperm, but not too thick to stop the good swimmers. After two and a half hours, Ericsson reported that ten per cent of the original sperm had swum to the bottom and, of this sample, 80 per cent were found to be Y sperm.

He has set up a company in California called Gametrics Ltd, which specializes in separating both human and animal sperm, and the technique is being used to prepare sperm to artificially inseminate women wanting sons. Unfortunately it cannot work with X sperm, because these are left behind at the top of the columns along with lots of dead sperm and debris which would not be suitable for artificial insemination. Ericsson says that 65 males and 19 females have been born using this method and, although two laboratories which tried to repeat his experiment at first could not make it work, a further six have since repeated it with success.

British scientists remain divided about the work, but most consider the ratio of Y to X sperm is not good enough to make it worth copying his work here with artificial insemination. Also, couples who were prepared to go to those lengths to conceive a son might have to be dissuaded from having the pregnancy terminated if it turned out to be a girl.

But how, you may be asking, did both Shettles and Ericsson know they had more Y sperm in their experiments, if those experiments were all about trying to find a way of telling the Y from the X? The answer lies in another, slightly less disputed but still controversial, test. This is to stain sperm with a dye called quinacrine which attaches itself to a spot on the Y chromosome. Under ultraviolet light this shows up as a brightly fluorescent spot — the X chromosome doesn't have this spot.

But the process is extremely difficult and results are very variable depending on the sperm sample. Some sperm react better than others, while some hardly react at all, and there's no chance of using this technique to separate samples of sperm for artificial insemination because it also kills them!

But work is going on to remedy that aspect — a remarkable step has been taken at the National Institute for Medical Research in London, where a biologist has discovered a dye that stains sperm to show a different pattern depending on whether they are X or Y and does not kill them.

Instead of penetrating the DNA molecules and damaging them, this new dye binds to the outside of the molecules. Obviously it will take many years of tests before we know if it is safe for use on humans, but it is an important breakthrough. So far, out of a dozen calves born, the ratio has been altered from the normal 1:1 to a 2:1 ratio and in rabbits an even better ratio of three and a half has been achieved.

Other attempts to separate the X and Y include sedimentation and centrifusion, to separate the DNA and see if the X proves heavier or larger. But again, the slight difference in the amount of DNA is outweighed by individual differences in the sperm.

Another theory was that the X and Y sperm might carry different electrical charges — if this was true, then putting them in an electrical field would make them move at different speeds. Some Japanese workers have claimed success recently but, again, they have used the controversial quinacrine staining to check results.

Treating sperm with antibodies has also been tried. We know that many women produce anti-sperm antibodies naturally, making them infertile or considerably lowering their fertility. But so far no one has discovered antibodies which can distinguish the X- from the Y-bearing sperm. Research is continuing.

Sperms have also been treated with chemicals and enzymes, tested to see if they give off an opposite electrical charge and subjected to reduced atmospheric pressure. The X and the Y remain stubbornly undivided.

But, tantalizingly, we do know that there *are* all sorts of factors

which can change the sex ratio very slightly, and one of these
— which we are most concerned with — is timing.

5.

A QUESTION
OF TIMING?

Is there really a time for girls and a time for boys — and if so, why doesn't it work for everyone?

This whole question has caused much head scratching amongst the scientific and academic world for many years. More than twenty papers have been published on the subject, but although many show that the time of conception makes a difference to the number of boys and girls born, the findings are sometimes contradictory.

The answer is that, yes, timing can make a difference. But exactly how, which mechanisms are being affected, and why, is still to be answered.

One of the problems is that there is no easy way to pinpoint the exact time of ovulation. Temperature charts — which we'll explain in Chapter 6 — can only show when ovulation has already taken place and, for lots of women, even that belated piece of information can be difficult to determine.

Fertility awareness — getting to know your own body so that you recognize the signs that ovulation is going to occur — can predict when ovulation is likely but unless you happen to be one of the 15 per cent of women who, it's reckoned, experience an actual twinge of pain when they ovulate, it still does not pinpoint the exact day.

So studies which rely first on women using a difficult and imprecise way of recording ovulation, and second on their ability to recall on which days of the month they had sex, can hardly be said to be working on reliable data!

Not surprisingly, therefore, lots of researchers have looked at results from artificial insemination because at least the keeping of temperature charts will have been supervised and there are records to show which days insemination took place. But the drawback is that couples going for artificial insemination already have a fertility problem that might upset some other mechanism which influences the sex ratio.

It was a New York gynaecologist in the fifties, an infertility specialist called Dr Sophie Kleegman, who found that artificial insemination on the day of ovulation meant 70 to 80 per cent more boys, and insemination two days or more ahead of ovulation meant more girls. Her findings — which agree with Hazel's theory — have been confirmed by other studies, although not all have found such a large swing towards boys.

So, using artificial insemination, a couple have a greater chance of having a boy if insemination is on the day of ovulation and a better chance of a girl if it is two or more days ahead. A clear formula for fertile couples to follow to conceive boys or girls?

Well, not according to some of the other findings because two studies looking at families able to produce children in the ordinary way, rather than by artificial insemination, claimed to show exactly the opposite! Namely, that girls are more likely to be conceived at the time of ovulation and boys ahead of ovulation — though it has to be said that the methods and data used in these studies have since been criticized.

One researcher, William James of University College, London, has pulled in these and many other findings to argue this theory and his suggestion is that the varying levels of certain female hormones through the cycle are responsible. But if his idea is right — that the reverse of Hazel's theory is correct — then we would certainly have expected to find far more disappointed families amongst her 100 guinea-pigs.

Certainly the whole question is fraught with many immeasurable variables and unknown factors. It could be, for example, that artificial insemination favours the Y sperm, but for reasons quite unconnected with the fact that they have a Y chromosome. Or perhaps the timing theory works only for some women, depending on their hormone levels. Perhaps having intercourse at a certain point after ovulation, when the body chemistry changes in ways we don't yet know, could be just as significant — perhaps for everyone or perhaps for the few.

Are there other factors which have been shown to change the basic ratio of boys and girls born? Yes, just a few! Consider these findings:

● More daughters are born to older mothers and older fathers.

● The more children you have the more likely you are to have girls.

● Women being treated with the fertility drug Clomiphene are more likely to have girls.

● Negroes have a slightly higher percentage of daughters than Caucasian races.

● Some disasters, such as flood, smog and hepatitis outbreaks, have been followed by a higher female birthrate.

● Anaesthetists seem to have more girls — and so do American fighter pilots.

● First babies are more often boys.

● During and after war there is a rise in the number of boys born.

● More boys are born during the first eighteen months of a marriage.

● The numbers of boys and girls born changes with the seasons — in America, June is the peak month for boys.

● In animal experiments trace elements selenium and arsenic have resulted in more males.

What Does it all Mean?

'Nothing at all, unless we can understand what causes these slight shifts,' was the weary verdict of one jaded academic.

Intriguing as they are, these alterations in the basic ratio of

105 or 106 boys for every 100 girls are only very slight and many hundreds of births have to be studied to be sure they even exist. More than that, the ways of linking cause with effect vary, and so do the results. Important factors can be missed because researchers don't know about them or don't have enough information. Nevertheless you have to be very incurious not to be tantalized by some of these findings, and academics continue to offer possible explanations.

Recently, for example, it has been suggested that a rise in the number of boys being born could act as an early warning system of some health hazard in our environment.

Armadale, a small industrial town in Scotland, was found to have had a cluster of deaths from lung cancer for the six years between 1968 and 1974. Air pollution from factories giving off metallic fumes containing iron, manganese and nickel was suggested as a possible cause. During the same period the number of boys born also rose very sharply.

It all poses many interesting questions in search of answers.

Of course, Hazel would be the first to agree that the families who have put her theory to the test hardly constitute a scientifically-based study. But in the face of so much uncertainty their results are just as thought-provoking as some research papers, especially when you consider the shaky material some academics went to print on!

6.

PINPOINTING OVULATION: PICKING 'EGGSACTLY' THE RIGHT TIME

Pinpointing ovulation is the trickiest part of the whole procedure, and the one that causes most problems. As we explained, there is no absolutely sure way, but nearly all women can have some success using one or all of the ways we describe here.

A woman's cycle runs from the beginning of one period to the beginning of the next period. The length of cycle varies from about 21 to 35 days in different women. Ovulation is most commonly thought to occur fourteen days *before* the next period, but there can be many variations even in a regular 28-day cycle, so just counting the days is not a good enough indicator.

A much better, but still imprecise, way of identifying the time of ovulation is by taking your temperature. The basal body temperature is your body's lowest daily temperature and is recorded first thing in the morning as soon as you wake up. It is very important not to eat or drink anything before taking your temperature because that will obviously change the reading.

Doctors used to recommend that women should not get out of bed before checking their temperature, but now Natural Family Planning teachers say that, as long as you put the thermometer in as soon as you wake, it doesn't make any difference if you get up and start to dress. Don't do anything strenuous though, like exercises, while taking the reading.

Leave the thermometer in for five minutes or, if you want

to take your temperature vaginally or rectally, allow three minutes. Basal body temperature is usually between 97.2° and 97.4°F (36.2° and 36.3°C). During menstruation it might be a bit higher, but start charting on day one of your cycle — the first day of a period — and just mark when bleeding finishes. Using a special fertility thermometer (details about where to get thermometers and charts are on page 82) makes things easier because the markings are bigger and don't have such a wide scale.

When ovulation has occurred, the temperature rises to a level of 98°F (36.7°C) or above — this is caused by the sharp rise in the levels of the hormone progesterone. This temperature rise also occurs in men if they are given an injection of progesterone. Sometimes, the day before this rise, there is a drop in temperature to its lowest level of the cycle. Remember that the rise in temperature does not mark ovulation itself — it only shows that ovulation has taken place. The day just before the rise is thought to be the time of ovulation but, obviously, the exact time must vary with individuals.

Mark off your temperature each day on your chart — lots of women ask their partners to do this for them. Even if your man is a bit sceptical about the whole idea, you need his co-operation and it won't hurt for him to understand a bit more about your body rhythms.

After ovulation your temperature stays raised until the start of the next period. If no period arrives and your temperature stays up, then congratulations, because you are probably pregnant!

When you join up the dots on your first month's chart don't expect to see a smooth line followed by an exact dip and rise to an equally smooth line at a higher level. Most people find that their temperature hops around quite erratically within that pattern and some women produce charts which are very hard to read. But the two halves of the cycle should be generally distinguishable, and if you study it you should be able to mark a recognizable start to the higher temperature in the second half.

It is important to be aware of other factors which can change your temperature — illness is an obvious one, but this rise is likely to be higher than that produced by ovulation. Taking pain-killers like aspirin can lower body temperature, which may mask ovulation. Too much alcohol, or even just a late night, can also send it rising unusually.

When you are keeping your temperature chart, think about how you feel each day — notice differences between fertile and non-fertile days. Getting to recognize signs that ovulation is about to take place is called fertility awareness.

The most obvious sign is a change in the mucus at the cervix, or neck of the womb. This is how Hazel found she could most easily recognize her fertile days. This change can be used as a method of natural family planning and is known as the Billings method after the doctor who first described it in 1972. Normally, the tiny canal through the cervix, called the os, is kept closed with a plug of mucus which sperms cannot penetrate. But, in the days approaching ovulation, the amount and consistency of this mucus changes to let sperms through.

If you put a finger to the entrance of your vagina each day you will probably find it feels quite dry early in the month. But about four days before ovulation — again, the time varies with each woman — the different mucus can be felt, either as just a sensation of wetness or as a clear jelly-like discharge with a rather stretchy consistency similar to egg white.

Another sign is a change in the position and condition of the cervix. Women who have used a diaphram as a contraceptive will know just what their cervix feels like and where to find it. But it's perfectly possible to go through all the experience of pregnancy and childbirth and still have no idea what really happens inside, especially if you've relied on a method such as the Pill as a contraceptive.

Lots of women have been brought up to feel it's wrong to touch themselves — if you feel a bit inhibited, try doing it in the bath. Slide a finger inside your vagina, feel as far along as you can towards your stomach. You should find a smooth lump — know-your-own body books describe it variously as feeling like a 'rounded cabinet knob', 'the end of your nose with a small dimple in it' or 'a chin with a dimple.'

Anyway, whatever you think it feels like, this is the cervix and, contrary to what some women imagine, it is not directly at the end of the vagina but protruding into the side, with the vagina extending to a closed end beyond. Nor does it stay in exactly the same place — during the non-fertile days it can be very low but it rises as much as an inch during the fertile phase.

So the position of your cervix is another indicator that ovulation is going to take place. If your fingers are sensitive you may be able to feel changes in the condition of the cervix itself — the os, the canal through to the womb, enlarges and softens.

Once you are able to distinguish the fertile days in your cycle, look out for any pain in the lower abdomen at about the time of expected ovulation. About 15 per cent of women are thought to experience this pain. This is how some women described the sensation: 'A very severe, one-sided pain — like a skewer being pulled through one ovary. More painful than a period and it lasts for a few hours. As I've got older it has become more marked.' . . . 'A twinge of pain low down and to one side — I feel it mostly in my back, a bit like a period pain.' . . . 'A little pain on one side which suddenly appears and fades off gradually. I realize I must have had it for years without noticing. I only became aware of it when I began to chart my fertility.'

Until you begin to know your own cycle it's hard to predict how far in advance of ovulation these changes take place — generally the build up of mucus starts about four days before ovulation, but that can vary. After ovulation lots of women notice differences in their body due to higher levels of progesterone — breasts feel fuller or more tender, and there may be a slight increase in weight or a feeling of being very slightly bloated because more fluid is being retained. These feelings accentuate towards a period, sometimes into the pre-menstrual syndrome from which many women suffer.

Pinpointing ovulation is much harder for some women than others but one teacher of natural contraception said in three years he had never met a woman who was unteachable.

Hazel's comment is: 'Be your own guinea-pig and be sensitive for any indication of ovulation — I'd like to hear from any readers who discover other ways of testing. Of all the methods of determining ovulation I think the personal one is the most straightforward and reliable, and it helps to learn more about your body's natural rhythm, for whatever reason.'

7.

CAN DIET MAKE A DIFFERENCE?

Can you eat your way to the baby of your choice? Several French doctors certainly think so and one in particular, Dr François Papa, an obstetrician at the Port-Royal Maternity Clinic in Paris, got together with journalist Françoise Labro to write a book about the diets.*

Dr Papa reports that, out of 155 women who tried the diet, 123 successfully conceived the sex of their choice. His journalist co-author, Françoise Labro, believes that following the diet gave her a son after two daughters. She echoed the sentiments of many women when she said: 'I felt I would be missing out on something if all my children were the same sex — and so would they.'

Françoise felt that, according to Dr Papa's theory, she didn't even have a fifty-fifty chance of conceiving a boy. Her natural eating habits followed the 'girl diet' almost exactly, which left her only a 20 per cent chance of having the son she wanted. Like Hazel, Dr Papa says he has had an 80 per cent success rate.

But can what you eat really change your body chemistry? Most scientists think not, pointing out that the body's cells have their own regulating mechanism which keeps the levels of such things as trace elements between a certain minimum and maximum.

Comments from British experts range from a blunt: 'There

* *Boy or Girl?* (Souvenir Press, 1984).

is no scientific evidence that diet has any bearing,' to: 'I'm not suggesting the doctors involved in this work are anything but totally sincere. But unless trials are conducted on an established scientific basis, and the findings published in recognized journals, these theories remain just that — theories.'

The basis of the diet theory is that four vital mineral salts in the body somehow influence whether an X or a Y sperm is most likely to fertilize the egg. These salts are sodium, potassium, calcium and magnesium.

For a girl a woman must follow a diet containing as much calcium and magnesium as possible — this means, amongst other things, drinking a lot of milk. For a boy she must eat a lot of sodium and potassium — this means eating as much salt as possible, an idea which has horrified health experts because all the evidence is that it may be the large amount of salt we already eat that is a contributory factor in many cases of high blood-pressure.

Nutritionists have attacked the diet on two grounds:

1.   That eating a lot of salt may be positively dangerous for some women — e.g., those predisposed to high blood-pressure.

2.   That following a restrictive diet before pregnancy could easily lead to eating an unbalanced diet — just at a time when eating plentiful supplies of all nutrients are essential to the health of your future baby.

Why do nutritionists advise us not to eat too much salt? After all, salt (the chemical sodium chloride) is vital to all living things. It regulates the fluid inside and outside the body's cells. In evolutionary terms this solution, which constantly moistens our tissues, is thought to be of about the same salinity as the sea from which mammals first emerged. 'Miniature oceans encased in skin,' is how one expert graphically described the human body.

But to do this job we only need one or two grams of salt a day — less than half a teaspoon. What we actually eat is a staggering ten to twelve grams a day, which amounts to more than two teaspoons.

That's because nearly all convenience foods contain a lot of salt — and not just savoury foods like crisps. Salt also lurks in large quantities in such products as instant chocolate pudding, most breakfast cereals and many cakes and biscuits. That's because there is sodium in baking powder as well as in preservatives (sodium benzoate and sodium nitrate) and flavourings (monosodium glutamate). And even vitamin C is often added in the form of sodium ascorbate. One cynic commented that most white loaves contain almost as much salt as flour because salt is cheaper!

There is no hard proof that too much salt causes high blood-pressure, but there is a great deal of circumstantial evidence. Certainly, putting a person with high blood-pressure on a low-salt diet always lowers the pressure, though drugs may be needed as well.

Doctors think that, while most of us can get rid of all this excess salt in sweat and urine, some people's bodies are lacking that safety mechanism. And high blood-pressure is such a common — and potentially fatal — condition that a general awareness of salt in the diet may help those people who are unaware they have a problem. Because, although high blood-pressure can cause strokes and heart attacks, the condition itself has no symptoms — you can only know if you have high blood-pressure by having it measured. Advice from nutritionists is simply to stop adding salt in cooking and break the habit of sprinkling it over food at the table. This will be enough to halve the amount you eat.

Certainly, with this kind of thinking around, it does seem unwise to step up your salt intake — and if most of us simply off-load the extra anyway it also seems pointless. The exponents of the diet theory themselves agree that just sprinkling an extra bit of salt over your meals or drinking more milk will not be enough to make a difference. Dr Papa and his team supervised the diets of the women taking part in minutest detail — and they also reinforced the mineral content with supplements.

Françoise Labro makes no bones about how hard it was to follow such a restrictive diet totally and exactly without deviation for, in her case, a year. Just before she finally conceived she wrote: 'Why carry on inflicting this kind of treatment on myself? I'm not that masochistic . . . I, who had hardly ever been greedy about food, dreamt of buns oozing with cream, gigantic plates of seafood loaded with oysters and lobsters; eggs, scrambled with truffles, hard-boiled with mayonnaise, poached on spinach, soft-boiled with brown bread, fried with bacon, in aspic with tarragon, or as an omelette with mushrooms . . .'

These are cravings that one British woman, who followed both the diet and also Hazel's timing theory, can sympathize with. Janet Fikri was so keen, after having four sons, to do anything to try and tip the balance in favour of a daughter that she thought she had nothing to lose by changing her diet as well as making sure she conceived ahead of ovulation.

For three months she charted her temperature and found it rose on the fourteenth day of each month. She also cut out tea, coffee and alcohol and drank only Perrier water or milk instead. She cut down on bread — but didn't cut it out completely which the diet recommends (unless it is unsalted) — and stayed off obviously salty food. Salt in cooking or on meals was also out.

'The hardest thing was giving up coffee,' says Janet. 'I love real coffee and usually drink about six cups a day. I switched to aniseed tea instead. My husband used to laugh at me and wave his cup of coffee under my nose! He didn't think it could make any difference.' But her husband changed his mind the day their fifth baby was born — Yasmin, at long last a sister for their lovely boys, Ian, Billy, Eden and Zak.

'I don't know if it was the diet or the timing — we definitely timed the conception to match Hazel's theory — that made the difference,' says Janet. 'But I believe that it was something we did and so does my husband, now.'

Diet or timing? Well even Janet did not follow the diet in

exactly the strict detail that Dr Papa's book recommends, nor did she take extra mineral supplements.

We would just say that if you really want to go in for the diet, read the book *Boy or Girl? Choosing Your Child Through Diet* so you know what's entailed and do not, on any account, try to work out your own diet without consulting your doctor first. We mentioned the risk of high blood-pressure and salt, but anyone with a family history of renal colic should not follow the calcium-rich (girl) diet. In addition, there is a real risk of eating an unbalanced diet, missing important nutrients, which could prejudice your baby's chances of optimum health. So make sure what you eat is adequately supervised, perhaps by the dietitian at your local hospital. For all parents, healthy babies matter more than the 'right' sex.

The Diet Theory: A Summary of Foods

Food for a boy:
As much salt as possible; tea; coffee; fruit juice; fizzy drinks; alcohol; salted butter; milk-free puddings and sauces; fresh or pre-cooked meat; all fish; one or two eggs a week. Rice; pasta; semolina; cornflakes; white bread and white-flour crispbread without milk; milk-free pastries and biscuits. All vegetables (except those listed as forbidden); all dried vegetables. All fresh fruit; dried prunes; raisins, dates, figs, chestnuts and apricots. Sugar; jam; fruit jellies and sorbets. Oils and milk-free margarine; olives; prepared soups and gherkins.

Forbidden food for a boy:
Milk in any form; all milk products (cheese, yogurt, etc.). Shellfish, molluscs (mussels etc.). Wholemeal bread, pastries and biscuits with milk. Salad vegetables; raw cabbage or cauliflower; spinach; cress. Nuts; cocoa; chocolate; mustard.

Food for a girl:
Milk (minimum 1⅓ pints/770ml a day); 4½ ounces (125g) of

meat or fish a day; eggs; unsalted butter; fresh cream; yogurt; unsalted soft cheese; milk puddings (twice a day as well as drinking milk). Salt-free bread and crispbread, and pastry without yeast or salt. Rice; pasta; semolina; tapioca; flour; cornflour. Limited amount of potatoes; fresh or frozen carrots; green beans; turnips; onions; leeks; peas; cucumbers; radishes; peppers; cress; celeriac; celery; salsify; cooked tomatoes; aubergines; green salad vegetables. Unsalted walnuts; hazelnuts; almonds; peanuts. Fresh, frozen or tinned apples, pears, clementines, strawberries, raspberries; tinned only pineapples, plums and peaches, all without syrup. Jam once a day; sugar; honey. Vegetable oils; pepper; spices; home-made sauces without salt. Perrier or Evian mineral water.

Forbidden food for a girl:

Salt and salt substitute in cooking or on foods; coffee; tea; chocolate; fresh or tinned fruit juice; fizzy drinks; wine; beer; cider; liqueurs; aperitifs; all pre-cooked meats; meat balls; fish fingers; salted, pickled or tinned fish; shellfish; roe; fish-cakes; anchovy paste; shrimp paste; all hard cheese; ordinary bread; pastries and biscuits unless salt-free as listed; sweetcorn; popcorn; crisps; parsley; spinach; cabbage; cauliflower; mushrooms; courgettes; endive; avocados; fennel; raw tomatoes; soya beans; dried peas and beans; dried fruit; fresh fruit (except those listed as allowed); chocolate and sweets; bicarbonate of soda; all prepared sauces; all preserves of vegetables; meat or fish outside the daily allowance; salted butter or margarine; ready made dishes whether tinned, fresh or frozen.

8.

HAZEL'S THEORY

If You Want a Boy

If You Want a Girl

Work out your ovulation dates in the way described in Chapter 6. Abstain from intercourse until the day of ovulation to make the sperm count higher. Have intercourse as close as possible to the time of ovulation or up to 24 hours later.

Work out your ovulation dates in the way described in Chapter 6. Have sex freely from the beginning of the cycle until three days before ovulation, then abstain or use a barrier method of contraception. If you don't conceive, gradually creep closer to the time of ovulation but don't get closer than 48 hours or you could end up with a boy!

Out of a hundred couples who tried Hazel's method, 81 got the boy or girl they hoped for and 19 did not. But, to confound the researchers who suggest that more people want boys than girls, by far the vast majority wanted girls. This was true of the failures as well as the successes — 14 had sons when they were hoping for girls and only five had girls and wanted sons.

And amongst the successes 56 wanted and got girls and only 25 wanted and got boys. All but one family already had one or more children and two families wanted the same sex — one wanted another boy and another wanted a second girl.

Nearly all the women charted their temperature in an attempt to pinpoint ovulation. The exceptions were a few who used only fertility awareness and some who used both this and the temperature.

Are There Couples Who Should Not Try Hazel's Method?

The answer is very definitely yes. There is no absolute guarantee of getting the right sex with Hazel's method, all it can do is tip the balance in favour of a boy or girl. Ask yourself these two questions:

- If you already had a boy or a girl, would you still be thinking about another baby?
- If the baby turned out to be the sex you hadn't hoped for, would you feel very disappointed?

If the answer to the first question is no, and to the second, yes, then think very carefully about having another baby. There have been families who seemed to follow Hazel's instructions carefully and despite this got the wrong sex. Since we do not know how or why the timing of intercourse in relation to ovulation makes a difference in the numbers of boys or girls born, there could be all sorts of reasons which can only be guessed at.

But individuals vary in every aspect of their body chemistry and, indeed, it would be very unusual if one formula could be found to work for everyone, especially in view of the fact that it is so hard to pinpoint the time of ovulation.

The families who tried Hazel's method were very loving, caring couples and nearly all made mention of how they wanted another baby anyway, whatever its sex.

This mother wrote: 'I have just given birth to a bouncing baby boy after trying for a girl. I am not disappointed, as he is lovely and his four-year-old brother is thrilled with him. I enclose a temperature chart of the month that I fell and it seems I timed everything quite correctly. Anyway, your book was very interesting and I love my son just the same!'

And this is a comment from an Australian mother of three sons: 'I tried for conception on day 13 and hadn't ovulated the next morning, but had on the morning of day 15. Nine months later our fourth son was born. Much as I love my four sons I'd love just one baby girl. I lent your book to five friends — three wanted boys and two wanted girls — and all were successful.'

Perhaps these mothers both ovulate closer to the rise in temperature so that intercourse was on the day of ovulation instead of ahead? Perhaps the mechanism — whether it involves hormone levels or some other aspect of body chemistry — works for some and not for others?

At the moment there's no way of knowing — all we do know is that all parents should be quite sure that they would love and want another baby whatever its sex.

9.

IT'S A GIRL!

The moment of birth is a miracle to every parent. You really can't believe that this huge, healthy baby has grown from just two tiny cells. And that natural drama and excitement is there with every birth — how ever many babies you have.

But for parents who have already seen one or more children into the world there is an added awareness that this is not just another new baby, but a personality that is going to make its mark on the life of the family. What kind of personality, only time will reveal. There are all kinds of children who grow into all kinds of adults. But for one moment, in the delivery room, there are only two kinds of babies — boys and girls. That moment only lasts a second or two and comes after concern about health and before that delicious time when parents begin to discover many other things about their new baby. But that revelation about the sex of your child is an instant, obvious piece of information you don't have to wait for.

And because every labour has the habit of wiping out the fog of maternal amnesia to bring back in sharpest detail the moments of other births, parents of two or more sons can begin to feel that one kind of baby is not for them; that baby girls are another experience, only to be watched in other people's lives. To find — after only boys — that they can actually produce girls seems to these parents like a miracle on top of a miracle!

'I was so excited I couldn't sleep all night — I couldn't believe I really had a daughter,' laughed Linda Lewington as she recalls how she felt the night she gave birth to a girl after two sons.

Susan McCormick and her husband Derek felt just the same when baby Jade made her entrance into this world. Experienced parents already, they had been delighted and thrilled to welcome Lee, Gary, Kevin and Derek but they did begin to think it was almost beyond belief that they would actually have a daughter.

'We wanted another baby anyway but I felt it was worth trying anything that might tip the balance in favour of getting a girl,' says Susan. 'I followed the instructions and I know I conceived early in the month. After four sons you can imagine how we felt when I finally gave birth to a daughter. It was like a dream come true.'

Isabel Audley is equally sure it was Hazel's timing theory that gave her Anne-Marie after three gorgeous sons, Matthew, Daniel and Thomas. As a former nurse, Isabel had some advantage when it came to reading temperature charts and, after ten months of temperature-taking, she was so expert at studying her own cycle that she could predict within half a day when she would ovulate. Her sons had all been conceived immediately but she was determined to give the theory every chance and not get closer than two days before ovulation. The result was a ten month wait before she got pregnant — a wait she now considers well worth while.

'We'd always wanted four children and I assumed, with that number, I was bound to get some boys and some girls. It was only after son number three that I began to think about it all. It seemed either I had to be out there kicking a football with them or I was on my own!

'My husband would have been quite happy with another son — it was me who specially wanted a daughter. But since she arrived she has brought us so much happiness — and it really is undoubtedly thanks to Hazel's method.

'The same goes for four good friends of ours, who all had two or more children of the same sex and have been successful in obtaining the desired sex of their child after following the theory very carefully.'

Catherine Warden tried Hazel's theory with an open mind about her chances of conceiving a boy or a girl but after three sons she and her husband felt they had nothing to lose. The result, after trying for conception two days ahead of ovulation, was a daughter — and something of a bonus for the previous generation as she was their first granddaughter after seven grandsons.

'It really has made a difference to our family, and especially to me,' says Catherine. 'After all, one woman living with four males is going to feel the odd one out sometimes.'

Judy and James Ramscar changed their diet as well as trying Hazel's method, but they just cut down on tea and coffee and Judy cut out salt as far as possible. Since the diet theorists say women have to follow every detail of the diet very strictly for it to work, it's doubtful if all this self sacrifice did in fact make much difference — although Judy may have benefited from the healthy reduction in salt. But she certainly made sure that she conceived this baby, her fourth after three sons, in the first half of the cycle by following four months of careful temperature taking. When a daughter duly arrived this is what she had to say: 'I feel having a daughter has made our family complete — and me especially happy. It really is a bonus.'

Another couple who felt their three healthy sons were smashing but that having a daughter too was the icing on the cake are Mary and Austin Gibbons. By charting her temperature Mary knew she tried for conception three days ahead of ovulation. She had an aminocentesis test during the pregnancy but didn't want to know her baby's sex until the birth.

Unlike most of the women surrounded by sons, Mary especially wanted a daughter for her husband. 'They do tend to say that a man isn't complete until he has a daughter,' she says — not a saying we can recall having heard, but certainly one to confound the researchers who maintain men want boys more than women!

Dr Alasdair Carter and his wife Yvonne are unusual in trying Hazel's method not just once but twice with success. They had two sons when they heard of Hazel's theory and decided to try it to see if it could bring them a daughter. To their delight it did and, when they went in for baby number four soon after, they repeated the formula to see if they could get an even set. They did, and although Yvonne now has her work cut out with two little girls as well as two growing boys, she is even talking about trying the boy formula for a fifth!

'I was already charting my temperature when I had the boys so I know they were conceived at ovulation or shortly afterwards,' says Yvonne. 'I tried for my first daughter four days before ovulation, but with the second we crept up to two days before ovulation. Of course it's a great help having my husband to interpret the charts, which I know some people don't find so easy.'

Yvonne is convinced that timing holds the secret to the sex of her children — her husband remains open-minded on the subject, but he thinks it's sufficiently intriguing to suggest it to some of his patients who are trying for a baby after having two or more of the same sex. 'It's certainly easy and harmless to try as long as couples are planning another baby anyway,' he says. 'We managed to get two girls after two boys using that method but there's no way of knowing if it was cause and effect.'

Ruth Bunce and her husband did the reverse of Dr Carter who suggested it to some patients, and were the patients who suggested it to their doctor — after following the method the couple had a daughter after two sons and their doctor had a boy after two daughters.

Joy and Malcolm Emms had a daughter after two sons — she said as a nurse she found it quite easy to work out her time of ovulation but, nurse's training or not, some people's cycles are very unpredictable. Linda Lewington found she could pinpoint ovulation by an actual pain she experienced and Kathryn Hill used the Billings method to conceive a daughter in the first half of her cycle after having had two sons. Indeed the Hills felt as though they'd broken a boys-only jinx when daughter Elizabeth arrived!

'We had two lovely sons but hoped that our third much-wanted baby would be a little girl,' says Kathryn. 'I conceived on the eleventh day of my cycle and, when it turned out to be a daughter, we were ecstatic! There were no girls on my husband's side of the family for generations back — we had broken the spell. The boys are delighted to have a sister and my husband and I have run out of superlatives to express how we feel.' A feeling all these families know only too well.

It can take longer to conceive a girl because trying too far ahead of ovulation means no conception at all. Zelda Lithgow was worried it would be a boy because she became pregnant immediately, as she had done with her two sons. But her temperature charts still showed it was ahead of ovulation and, sure enough, she got her girl.

But whether a woman uses a temperature chart, the Billings method or just personal knowledge of her body's rhythm to pinpoint ovulation, it does take two to get the timing right! Men are generally inclined to be more sceptical, at least early on, but they've got to be willing to co-operate, otherwise love-making by the calendar could lead to divorce instead of the baby of your choice.

'You've got to be relaxed and not nag your husband,' points out Annette Carroll, who became pregnant on the eleventh day of her cycle to give birth to a longed-for daughter after two equally adored boys. Wise advice indeed.

10.

IT'S A BOY!

As you've read, there have been lots of large families with only boys who wanted, and got, a daughter. The families who only had girls and were keen to have a son were both fewer in number and smaller — so far Hazel has had no cases with more than two daughters. But, just like the 'boy' families, the 'girl' families all wanted another baby anyway, whatever the sex, and felt it would be an extra dimension if they could have a boy.

In theory it should be easier to try for a boy because it just means pinpointing ovulation instead of trying to forecast when it is likely to happen. But it still needs careful temperature-taking and fertility awareness, as Viv Austin found out. She had heard that ovulation takes place on the fourteenth day and that boys were more likely to be conceived then, and followed that plan for her second child who turned out to be a much-loved second daughter.

'Then I read about Hazel Phillips and sent for her book,' says Viv. 'When I followed her advice and began charting my temperature, it didn't take long to notice that I didn't ovulate until the sixteenth day.' Viv made sure she conceived her third baby on the day of ovulation and the result, nine months later, was a lovely boy to join sisters Lauren and Emma.

And Elizabeth Caush found her ovulation day was the fifteenth not the fourteenth in her cycle — she already had a daughter and was delighted when following Hazel's plan brought her a boy recently.

Jan and Christine Newman had two girls of four and six when

they decided to have another child.

'We wanted another baby anyway and did not mind a third girl, but we decided it would be fun to try and change the odds towards a boy,' says Christine. 'I must admit that, having got pregnant immediately with both the girls, I did find the temperature-taking quite tedious — I'm hopeless in the morning anyway and there were times when I felt like throwing the thermometer out the window!'

But, fortunately, her husband has plenty of patience as well as a physicist's good head for figures and helped her with the charting. Naturally they were both delighted when their efforts at getting the timing right were rewarded nine months later with a boy. 'I'm convinced it's because he was conceived at the time of ovulation,' says Christine. 'We'd like a fourth son and we shall definitely try the same plan to see if we can get another boy.'

Judith Wardley is also firmly convinced that it was timing that gave her and her husband their son Christopher after daughters Emma and Cassie. 'I would never have tried anything which involved taking drugs but Hazel's method was easy and natural,' says Judith. 'Both sexes of children give us great pleasure and I am so pleased to have had the chance of both.'

Carol Paterson was one of those who found, after keeping a temperature chart, that she didn't ovulate on the same day each month. But Carol managed to learn the signs that meant ovulation was near and she was lucky to be amongst the minority of women who actually experience a slight passing pain at ovulation that enabled her to pinpoint the right time. Nine months later she was able to give Hazel the good news that she and her husband had a boy, James, a brother for Lorna and Susan. 'I still can't believe I've actually got my son,' she wrote three weeks after the birth.

Catherine and Peter Gates went in for Hazel's method not too seriously — which is probably the best approach — although they did follow the instructions carefully. Naturally both of them were over the moon when it did give them a son.

And, just as with the families who had boys and wanted girls, those couples who only wanted two children or could only have two were just as delighted if they managed to get one of each.

Julia Taft was unlucky enough to suffer from postnatal depression after her first child, a daughter, was born. The memory was still with her when she went in for her second, and both she and her husband felt they didn't want more than two children. 'I really was very keen to get a boy,' says Julia. 'I followed the special diet, eating more salty things and cutting dairy products, I charted my temperature and also invested in an electronic gadget called *Ovin* which records your body's electrical charge. I even got books to work out my biorhythms!'

Julia knew that her daughter had been conceived early in the cycle because she was an accident — though one they have been delighted and thrilled with ever since. This time they made sure their second child was conceived on the day of ovulation and when they did succeed in getting a little boy, both Julia and Robert were ecstatic.

'I cannot tell you what a thrill it has been to have a little boy to follow a daughter — we have not come down to earth yet,' said Julia at the time, and even a couple of years later still admits to being thrilled at the thought that they chose their son.

Linda Hall also knew she did not want more than two children and, like Julia, conceived a daughter first by accident. 'I didn't want a big family and as I had a caesarian section with my first child, a girl, my doctor advised me to have only one more,' she says. Her husband, Eric, was sceptical about their chances of success, but went along with Linda because he felt they had nothing to lose. But three months of careful temperature charting and conception on the day of ovulation gave the Halls the mixed family they had hoped for.

11.

SHOULD WE TRY TO CHOOSE THE SEX OF OUR CHILDREN?

How much do you want a boy or a girl? Enough to buy this book, yes. Perhaps enough to try timing the conception? Or to follow a difficult and possibly hazardous diet for two months? Even to try and arrange a test to tell you the baby's sex early in pregnancy? Enough to actually go so far as to have an abortion if the baby wasn't the gender you wanted?

Sex selection — both now and in the future when a method of pre-selection is discovered — raises all kinds of moral, ethical and feminist issues to which there are no easy answers.

At present, the only sure way of getting a boy or a girl is to have either a chorionic biopsy in the ninth week of pregnancy or an amniocentesis test in the sixteenth week and then an abortion if it turns out to be the wrong sex. That this sometimes already happens seems certain, although we can't know if doctors are genuinely misled, or suspect the true motives for a couple's inquiry but go ahead without asking too many questions. In theory, a couple could go to one doctor to ask for a test pretending they were anxious about the risk of genetic disease and, once they had discovered the sex of the baby, go to another doctor and ask for an abortion for equally bogus psychological or social reasons.

Amongst those who agree with abortion there are many shades of opinion. Some agree with it only if the health of the mother or baby is at risk. But even when tests show the baby will be born with some defect, there are still shades of grey. The tests often can't show the extent of the damage — no one can predict how much can be repaired and what kind of life the child and parents can expect.

Many people believe that abortion should be freely available because it is wrong for a woman to have to give birth to a baby she does not want. The view within the feminist movement is also that women should have control over their own bodies. But what happens to the feminist argument when a woman decides she doesn't want to give birth to a baby because it is a boy, and she only wants a girl? Or does that depend on her reasons for making that choice? A culture where women are second-class citizens, with boy babies valued and prized and girl babies unwanted and rejected, may be an open and shut case. What about a single woman who wants a baby, as many do, and feels only equipped to bring up a daughter because there would be no father around to offer a role model to a son?

That it should ever be acceptable for couples to abort babies just because they are the wrong sex might seem hard to imagine, but society does change its mind over many issues. Certainly it is true that people do care about the sex of their children and do have preferences. We know this from history, from modern surveys and from the response to any suggestions that a technique for choosing the sex of children has been discovered.

But how strong that preference is, and how far people are prepared to go to see it realized, is obviously very variable. There is a vast difference between a couple who have two or more children of the same sex, want another baby anyway, and would like to try something not too difficult in an attempt to tip the balance in favour of a child of the opposite sex and the couple who have no children and who want not only a particular number of boys or girls but also arranged in the right order.

At the moment, amniocentesis and abortion is only considered acceptable as a way of sex selection when there is a risk of sex-linked genetic disease. This is a disease such as haemophilia or Duchenn muscular dystrophy which can be carried by both men and women but only physically affects men. Parents known to be carriers obviously want daughters because they will be free of the illness.

But if ordinary, healthy couples began to use the practice for sex selection, there would be various consequences. One is that an extra burden would be placed on medical facilities, and women needing this kind of genetic screening because of their age or medical history would find it harder to get help. Inevitably, those rich enough to buy these kind of services would fare best. And a back-lash from the anti-abortion movement could be predicted, making it harder for women to get abortions for other reasons. How successful the movement would be in changing the law on abortion would depend largely on the government in power.

In Britain, Margaret Thatcher's government appointed a philosopher, Dame Mary Warnock, to chair an Inquiry to consider the ethical and moral questions raised by new technology which has made test-tube babies, surrogate mothering and frozen embryos a reality. Amongst the many difficult issues they considered, the committee also discussed sex-selection. Not surprisingly they were in favour of a method — if it could be developed — being offered to couples with good medical reasons for wanting to choose the sex of their child, i.e., to avoid hereditary sex-linked diseases. On the present position they had this to say:

> It seems possible that, as a result of the present research in this field, in the not too distant future, a reliable and simple method of selecting the sex of a child before fertilization will be developed. The apparatus for carrying out such a procedure could well be marketed commercially for self-administration. This seems to us to be an important area of concern. As we understand the current position, there is a possibility that certain types of 'do-it-yourself' materials for gender selection would not come within the ambit of the Medicines Act 1968. We consider it essential that the public should be protected from any such kits that do not actually possess the qualities claimed for them and therefore recommend that all types of 'do-it-yourself' sex-selection kits should be brought

within the ambit of control provided by the Medicines Act with the aim of ensuring that such products are safe, efficacious and of an acceptable standard for use.

In other words, no unscrupulous entrepreneurs should be allowed to make a fast buck out of preparations which don't work or, worse still, are dangerous — though a 'do-it-yourself' sex-selection kit does sound rather a lonely business, not to say a contradiction in terms!

Certainly Hazel's method is totally natural and not a 'kit' — it is merely a question of following the woman's natural cycle and choosing the right day for intercourse. There is no fussing about with creams or preparations — and, provided you want another baby anyway, you'll be no worse off than if you hadn't tried.

But the Inquiry also looked at another important aspect of the whole question — would a way of choosing the gender of our children upset nature's careful balance of the sexes and how would that affect the role of women in our society?

12.

WILL NATURE'S BALANCING ACT BE UPSET?

You don't have to be one of those types who only dresses girl babies in pink or tells their sons that boys don't cry, to care about what sex your children are. Friendships with people are influenced by whether they are the same or the opposite sex, just as much as they are by personality, age and a multitude of other factors.

How many of the differences between men and women are because of their biological make-up and how many to do with social conditioning is a complex argument, and we will look at the differences in the way we treat boys and girls in the next chapter. But, if you care about freedom for both men and women, perhaps it's more important to accept that there are as many similarities as differences between the sexes and that, when it comes to the differences, not all men and women have to be different in the same way.

Certainly — whether because of conditioning or biology — the balance of the sexes does influence family life. 'Complete' is the word that came up again and again when the couples who tried Hazel's theory were asked to describe what difference a mix of sexes had made to the family.

What also came across was the balanced, rational view of the whole business that these couples had. Nearly all of them already had one or more children of the same sex and wanted another baby anyway. They thought there was no harm in trying for one of the opposite sex but above all they wanted a healthy baby which they were prepared to love and welcome whatever its sex.

But, if there was a guaranteed, easy way to choose the exact composition of a family, would this balanced, rational view persist amongst the general population? All the studies and surveys that have been done come up with the finding that more people want boys — this varies from just a mild preference through to a positive obsession.

As you'd expect, the desire for boys is strongest in developing countries where the economy is still tied to agriculture. If a family lives largely off the land then sons can actually mean a better standard of living. And in countries where women are still second-class citizens their worth is often measured by their ability to produce sons. Some Indian men see a ratio of three to five boys for every girl as about right!

In both developed and developing countries it is men who are more likely to want boys, but in those countries women often want sons mainly to please their husbands.

In China there is a government campaign to control the population by offering incentives and rewards to parents who only have one child, and exerting heavy pressure on couples who try to have more. We don't know how widely sex selection is practised there, but a preference for boys and an acceptance that parents can abort on the grounds of sex selection has been indicated. The authorities are also more likely to turn a blind eye to rural families having two children, because it is accepted they need a son to work on the land.

You might think urban England has outgrown the need to produce sons to work on the land but, amongst Hazel's families, there were in fact two who wanted sons either partly or largely to take on farms — in both cases they already had two or more daughters.

Our preference for boys or girls changes as we get older, studies have shown. Small children are in no doubt — one like themselves cannot be bettered, as anyone who has ever spent time in an infant playground, and listened to the occasional outbreaks of 'boys are best' or 'girls are best' arguments, can testify.

But older children are much more likely to say they'd like to have a boy, and so are college students. By the time we've become parents preference has lessened because, by now, half of us have daughters, but it hasn't completely disappeared.

Some researchers have suggested that, after an initial swing towards boys, the scarcity of girls would mean a swing in the opposite direction and that eventually we'd settle back into a fifty-fifty ratio. But nature's balance may have many subtle checks and balances of which we are unaware — that there is elasticity in the design is shown by the fact that more boys are born during and after wars, for example, though no one knows why. Tampering with the balance could have repercussions we could never predict.

As well as simply the numbers of boys and girls, there is also the question of birth order. The traditional story-book version of family life with two children, a boy first and then a girl, is still the most popular. Would we find ourselves with a pattern of aggressive, over-ambitious first-born males and submissive, second-born females? And what would such a pattern do for the equality of the sexes? Very little, is the short answer, quite apart from being extremely dull. The Warnock Inquiry put it like this:

> It is often suggested that a majority of couples would choose that their first child was male, and if this happened, it could have important social implications, since there is considerable evidence that the firstborn sibling may enjoy certain advantages over younger siblings. It would have particular implications for the role of women in society, although some would argue that these effects would today be less damaging than they might have been a hundred years ago. These important considerations make the Inquiry dubious about the use of sex-selection techniques on a wide scale, but because of the difficulty of predicting the outcome of any such trend we have not found it possible to make any positive recommendations on this issue.

The Inquiry concluded that the whole question of sex selection should be kept under review. Because such Inquiries need the feedback of public opinion in the end to help them make decisions, it might pay all of us to look beyond the confines of our own desires and consider what sex selection might mean for society in general.

The pros and cons of sex selection and its effects were debated in a collection of essays by mainly American researchers and academics in a book called *Sex Selection of Children* and these are some of the points they made.

In Favour	Against
1. Sex-linked diseases could be avoided.	1. Sex selection might be open to only the rich.
2. Balanced two-child families would be possible.	2. It might lead to an imbalance of the sexes, with more boys.
3. Happier families.	3. There would be a concentration of first- and second-born characteristics in boys and girls.
4. Fewer unwanted children.	
5. The status of women in some developing countries would improve because girls would have to be specially chosen and wanted.	4. There could be social and unforseen long-term consequences of changing the sex ratio.
6. Better population control.	5. It might set a precedent for genetic engineering, i.e., trying to produce a super breed of only intelligent or gifted babies.
7. Better family planning.	
8. More human control over genetics.	6. More conflict between the sexes.
	7. Potential political abuse.

Do those arguments all seem a bit far removed from the mother with two sons who just thinks, idly, that it might be nice to take a wander through the girls' clothes department for a change? Certainly, judging by the response and comments from the people who have tried Hazel's methods, an awful lot of you wouldn't be too keen on a guaranteed way of choosing the sex of a first baby.

It would surely make for a dull, boring world to have virtually all families tailored the same, and lots of people who start out with the conventional, story-book view of first a boy and then a girl subsequently find there's a lot to recommend a completely different type of family.

The trouble with discoveries is that you can't unlearn them. Let's hope future generations are sensible enough not to want only identikit families.

13.

SEX-STEREOTYPING: BOYS WILL BE . . . ?

Boys will be boys and girls will be girls but — according to the sociologists — that's just because we make them like that.

In a totally equal society, so the theory goes, girls would be just as likely to be footballers, to be mad about cars or to want to get to grips with real tool sets. Boys would be equally delighted with dressing dolls, fiddling round with each other's hair or pottering about in the kitchen.

It's the old 'nature versus nurture' argument and, in fact, the truth is that it's very hard indeed to tell just what is conditioning and what does come down to natural differences between the sexes.

Consider some of these stories from parents: 'I bought my first child, a girl, a set of plastic cars from Mothercare when she was about 18 months old but, despite my attempts to interest her, she just never played with them.

'Yet from the age of about one my second child, a boy, used to crawl around with one of these cars under his hand making "brrmm, brrrm" noises. I honestly didn't present them to my daughter as boring and to my son as fascinating, yet that's the way they reacted.'

And this mother with a boy first and a girl second found the same thing: 'My son was mad about cars and the house was littered with them — my daughter also had the model to copy of my eldest child continually playing with them.

'Yet, although she copied him in many other ways, she didn't have the slightest interest in the cars — I had certainly expected her to like them and offered them as playthings so I really think I didn't give her any messages that they were "boys'" toys'.

Parents told more stories about games boys played that left girls cold, than the other way around. Cars, mechanical fiddling with tools or electronic bits of junk and football were most often mentioned as things in which girls never showed any interest. But feminists and sociologists would say that's just because we condition our children from day one — without even realizing we're treating them differently. There's no answer to that, is there?

An experiment at Sussex University apparently showed just this. Boys and girl babies of six months old were presented to mothers as either their true, or the opposite, sex, dressed in appropriate pink or blue clothes. The mothers played with and talked to them differently, depending on whether they thought they had 'John' or 'Jane'.

If they'd been told it was a boy they responded to any vigorous physical activity by encouraging more of the same — so, when the baby kicked or made a big movement they might bicycle his legs or jump him up and down. They hardly ever did this with the babies they had been told were girls. What the mothers said also encouraged this difference and, when they were asked to pick a toy for the baby from both neutral and sex-typed toys, number one favourite for the boys was a rubber hammer and for the girls a soft animal toy.

Leaving aside what we're doing to our children without realizing it, there are still lots of parents who quite consciously expect, and even demand, different behaviour from their sons and their daughters.

'He's a real little boy — quite different from the girls,' said one mother of a five-month-old who can't honestly have evinced much evidence of the macho spirit yet, making it sound as though he was ripping his mobiles to shreds and tearing up his cot mattress!

And lots of pre-school children can list whole categories of things girls or boys do or don't do — from wearing red shoes (not for boys apparently) to climbing trees (still barred to girls in some parts of the country it appears!)

Children whose parents do try to give them a non-sexist upbringing can still be made painfully aware that the rest of the world doesn't share that view. 'My two children had some money to spend and we went to choose a small toy each,' recalled the mother of a six-year-old son and a four-year-old daughter. 'My daughter wanted a Flower Fairy doll which had been advertised on television and — though presumably the ad had been directed at girls — my son was also attracted to the Flower Fairy and was torn between that and a "Dungeons and Dragons" figure.

'In the end he whispered to me: "If I have a Flower Fairy you won't tell the shop lady that it's for me will you?" I think that's very sad.'

And another mother met with a similar attitude from this shop assistant: 'We went to buy a Poochy Dog as a present for my daughter who was in hospital. It's a soft white dog with pink ears. My son, who was going to give it to her, took it up to the counter to pay.

'The assistant looked at him in horror and said: "You can't have that, that's a girl's toy!" In fact my son would have been just as delighted with it and asked me if it really was just for girls.'

Lots of toy shops obviously put their sensitive assistants through some kind of sex-typing of toys test before they let them loose on the customers!

Advertising has just as much to answer for — all parents can testify how much children can be influenced by seeing some craze promoted on the television. But until someone tries showing boys collecting Sindy's wardrobe and girls roaring around on the latest BMX bike we won't know how much our children's choice of toys is directed by what we think the different sexes should like, and what they naturally go for.

School seems to mark a big divide between the sexes. This mother with three sons and then a daughter said: 'My youngest son loved playing with dolls and we bought him a pram to push around. But once he went to school he stopped all that and now he's seven he won't believe he did play with dolls, except that I've got photos to prove it. I think it's a shame they feel they have to do "boy's" things all the time — after all we wouldn't laugh at a man pushing a pram would we?'

Quite a lot of mothers said there wasn't necessarily so much difference in what the boys and girls played as how they played — noise, lots of rushing around and physical action were far more common with boys. The girls were more inclined to play with just one other child in a game that involved lots of setting out and arranging.

Even the workers at a nursery in North London which tries to run on non-sexist lines said that the boys took up far more space than the girls — rushing around being Batman was their number one favourite game, which the girls didn't join in very often.

And lurking behind very many parents' attitudes towards what kind of behaviour is appropriate for boys or girls, is the fear that the boy who plays with dolls will turn out gay and the girl who doesn't like pretty clothes or dolls will end up being undesirable to men. Worries about lesbianism seem less prevalent than homosexuality. 'Tomboy' is often used affectionately, while 'cissy' is only ever used as an insult.

Are parents who specially want a girl or a boy more likely to try and stereotype their children's behaviour? One argument is that, in wanting a boy or a girl, they inevitably want someone who will behave in the way they consider a boy or girl should. Thus, the parents of a 'chosen' son who grows up to be a ballet dancer or of a daughter who becomes a wrestler will be disappointed. But, taken one stage further, this becomes a sexist argument in itself — the presumption being that those roles really aren't suitable for those sexes and thus the parents will be disappointed.

There is also an argument to be made that children in single-sex families may be subjected to less sexual stereotyping because the minority parent will make more effort to interest them in pastimes he or she might otherwise share with a child of their own sex.

Measuring natural differences between the sexes is obviously very difficult. But there seems some agreement amongst specialists who have studied the subject, that girls talk better and sooner, while boys show more aggression, are better at maths and show more visual-spatial ability. There's also been a suggestion that girls who were exposed to extra doses of male hormones in the womb — either because of an imbalance or to try and prevent miscarriage — are more likely to be aggressive and not play with dolls so much.

Certainly our society is beginning to have far less rigid ideas about what is the right way for men and women to behave. If sex choice ever became a 100 per cent reality, let's hope sex-change operations wouldn't take off as the latest way for rebellious teenagers to flout their parent's authority!

14.

POINTS FROM HAZEL'S POSTBAG

'I have one daughter, aged three, and my wife and I would like another baby — we want to follow your theory to try for a boy but I wonder if I may only have female-producing sperm?'

Hazel's answer: 'This worry is typical of the torments people think up for themselves and brood over in their minds. I had similar thoughts when our second daughter came along, and I still leap to equally unreasonable conclusions sometimes over emotionally fraught problems. But it is one of the blessings of middle age that experience makes me less ready to assume I am abnormal or unique; invariably someone else has been there before! The whole subject of sex, from whatever aspect, is so important to everyone and so emotive that perspectives are easily lost. But if you read Chapter 2, about the X and Y sperm, you will see that both result from a full set of chromosomes dividing — it would be very rare indeed for a man to have more of one type of sperm than the other.'

'I have four sons and, amongst my friends, know far more cases of large families of boys than girls. Why do some people seem to have only one sex?'

Hazel's answer: 'The most common reason, it seems, for an initial run of boys is that the woman has learned (correctly) that ovulation is the most fertile time of the month, when she is most likely to conceive. Wanting a baby, she therefore heads for the day of ovulation and produces boy after boy! Those with a more random approach, like me, just enjoy sex from the start of the cycle without calculating the most likely time for ovulation and therefore are more likely to produce girls to begin with. But of course since we don't know exactly which mechanism is being affected and why, there may be other factors at work we don't yet understand. But in the case of families with several children of one sex there are many examples, as you have read, to show that this trend can be reversed.'

'Do you think sperm count can affect the chances of producing a boy or a girl?'

Hazel's answer: 'A low sperm count obviously makes it more difficult to conceive a baby of either sex but there has been some suggestion that more girls are born to older fathers — when you might expect fertility to be declining — and more boys to couples who have only been married eighteen months or less, whom you might expect to be younger with a higher level of fertility. A man's sperm count is certainly variable, and is affected by such things as drinking, illness and temperature. Over-heating of the testicles definitely reduces sperm count — try loose boxer shorts and (heroic!) cold sponging of the genitals to raise the level, and frequent sex and warmth to lower it. Close-fitting pants or a jock-strap lowers sperm count temporarily. Dr Shettles' research indicated that low sperm count usually results in the conception of a girl.

'My doctor was absolutely horrified when I asked him about the chances of trying to get a boy or a girl baby — he made me feel it was wrong of me even to want a particular sex.'

Hazel's answer: 'I don't know why some doctors should take this attitude towards one of the most natural longings that nearly all parents have at some time or another. Of course they would be right to counsel couples who *only* want a boy or a girl against trying for another baby, just as we have done. It's also reasonable to expect that doctors, working to prevent or cure illness, should mainly be concerned with the chances of producing a healthy baby and methods which could prejudice this — such as odd diets — are obviously an anathema to them. But not all doctors feel like this and many, confronted by sane, intelligent parents who want another baby anyway and would like to see if they can tip the balance, are sympathetic and helpful. Some have even been sufficiently open-minded to try it themselves, as you have read.'

'My husband is in the Navy and away for long stretches of time. When he is home it's lovely and rather like another honeymoon all over again — but it doesn't always fit in with temperature charts and abstaining for a week before the day of ovulation.'

Hazel's answer: 'Lots of women have mentioned this problem, when their husband's job takes them away even for short stretches of time — for example, pilots, lorry drivers and sales reps. I think the best plan is just to use a sheath or cap if it isn't the right time and, above all, to be relaxed about the whole business — don't turn sex into a chore to be performed at the right time!'

'Can having an orgasm make a difference to the chance of getting a boy or girl? I never have an orgasm with my husband. I just lie back and enjoy it as much as possible but it's honestly not all that wonderful.'

Hazel's answer: 'When women write like this I feel sad and wish they could enjoy one of the greatest pleasures I know. Their husband's pleasure would be doubled and their sex life would be more fun for both of them. When I got married, I don't think I had ever heard of a *woman* having an orgasm — I thought sex was just something men seemed to enjoy doing and their wives had to put up with. Fortunately I married a very unselfish man who didn't enjoy sex fully by himself, but wanted me to enjoy it as much as he did. He was sure that I could reach orgasm too so he spent a long time exploring my body and finding out how to give me pleasure. Today most young women expect to enjoy sex as much as their partners, but from the letters I get there are still many women who find it hard. Talk to your partner and don't be embarrassed or shy about enjoying sex. The Marriage Guidance Council offers sex counselling to couples at many centres and there are a multitude of books on the subject. But in reply to your question about whether orgasm influences sex determination the answer seems probably not much. Dr Shettles thought it could change the pH factor of the vagina but no research has showed acidity or alkalinity of their environment changes the way in which sperms behave. Ancient Jewish tradition, as recorded in the Talmud, holds that female orgasm favours the conception of a boy (*Tohoroth: Niddah*). But it also states cleanliness rules which delay the post-menstrual resumption of intercourse for two weeks — which brings the time, in a regular 28-day cycle, up to the day of ovulation! I think that it is *this* factor which produces the boys. So, don't ruin your love life by worrying!

'Do you think that hormone levels could play a part in determining the sex of a baby?'

Hazel's answer: I think, in agreement with the research done by Dr Ash of the College of Alternative Medicine and Science, Cornwall, England, that the determination of sex could well be due to the changing levels of the hormones oestrogen and progesterone in a woman's menstrual cycle. Post menstruation (and before ovulation) is the female-type oestrogen hormone phase, and prior to menstruation (after ovulation) is the male-type progesterone hormone phase; and at the interphase ovulation occurs.

'I've heard there are several types of equipment available to help confirm ovulation date. Could you tell me what they are and what you think of them?'

Hazel's answer: 'There are many gadgets on the market to help you find your ovulation day. They can be very useful to women who find it difficult to pinpoint this crucial event. To help you with the temperature-taking chore:

Temperature Charts: Available from most chemists, either singly or in booklets. 1992 price: 58p for ten. Published by:

G. H. Zeal Ltd.
Lombard Road
Merton
SW19 3UU
(Tel: 0181-542 2283/6)

These are very clear and easy to follow.

Temperature charts can also be obtained from The Family Planning Association (FPA) at local centres or at these addresses. 1992 price: 26p for six:

27 Mortimer Street
London
W1N 7RJ
(Tel: 0171-636 7866)

St Patrick's Health Centre
Highgate Street
Birmingham
B12 0YA
(Tel: 0121-440 2422)

The Health Centre
Blackbird Leys Road
Oxford
(Tel: 0865 755186)

These FPA charts are not quite so good for sex determination purposes. They are primarily concerned with *contraception* and so indicate fertile and non-fertile times in the monthly cycle. But, speaking from my own experience, I do not fully trust the 'safe' period!

Fertility Thermometers: Available at most chemists. Also from G. H. Zeal Ltd. These are easier to read than the old clinical thermometers because they give the temperature markings in larger divisions, which are easier for early-morning bleary eyes to focus on.

Electronic digital thermometer: There are many digital thermometers on sale today from chemist shops. They are much quicker and easier to read than old mercury thermometers.

Digital thermometers flash your temperature on to a small display panel for you to read and record. It is simple to plot a chart from such readings.

Fertility kits: Also on the market are a number of 'Fertility Kits' which give us warning of ovulation. Two of them are called 'First Response' and 'Clearplan'. A friend of mine tried out First Response and found it worked accurately. I have since heard that Clearplan is even simpler to use.

These chemical tests measure a woman's Luteinizing Hormone (LH) which peaks 36 hours *before* ovulation thus giving a useful warning of this event.

When the test swabs turn bluest, it is a sign that ovulation will take place 36 hours later.

Remember, this test does not indicate ovulation itself but gives a warning that it is imminent.

Read the instructions!

Electronic method: I used a neat little electronic gadget called *Ovin*. This enables a woman to tell when she is ovulating by registering a positive electric charge when she holds it against her skin above the knee. Usually the reading is negative, but the body's electric charge changes at ovulation and gives a positive reading. *Ovin* has been designed to measure this electric charge generated by the body, and by taking readings morning and night, a woman can find out exactly when she ovulates. This method proved a reliable indicator of ovulation for me during the three years that I was experimenting with it.

POSTSCRIPT

MY HOPES FOR THIS BOOK
Hazel Phillips

I feel the greatest achievement of this book will be in any contribution it makes to checking one of the most menacing problems of our time — the population explosion. Few would wish to see such a drastic solution as the Chinese have put into practice, which is a limit of one child per couple. Yet I do feel very many families would have fewer children if they could choose a mixture of the sexes, and that is probably especially true in developing countries.

You think I am exaggerating the threat posed by the growing world population? Then listen to the tale of the water lily:

A farmer had a big pond for fish and ducks. On the pond was a tiny lily. This tiny lily was growing. It was doubling in size every day. 'Look,' said the people to the farmer, 'you had better cut this back. One day it will be so big that it will kill all your fish and ducks.'

'All right, all right,' said the farmer. 'But there's no hurry. It is only growing very slowly.' The lily carried on doubling in size every day. 'Look,' said the farmer. 'It is still only half the size of the pond. No need to cut back yet.'

The next day, the farmer had a big surprise . . .

I feel that the water lily of human fecundity is approaching the half-way mark: Why do we not cut back? In the past poor contraceptive methods took the question out of our control. But now we must look to other reasons — religious, socio-economic, personal and political.

The desire for children of one or other sex is an important

aspect. No one should be ashamed of such a desire — it is the most natural wish in the world. But we should try to ring the changes with a smaller number of offspring.

My own grandmother was bringing up six sons. She prayed and prayed for a daughter. When she fell pregnant again, she hoped and hoped for a daughter. She ended up with — twin sons!

If one of those six boys had been a chosen girl, her family might have been much smaller. I would urge all women to choose their children, and then stop!

At the beginning of this book you will have read that I suffer from an illness for which science cannot yet find an answer — multiple sclerosis. My own doctor is one of the best and he says frankly to me: 'You know there is nothing I can do for you. No cure. The only thing is management.' And this is what he helps me with, as do all the useful gadgets for the disabled.

How to choose the sex of your baby is also a problem which science cannot yet answer. So what I am offering is also the art of management. Although we none of us have all the answers or the proof, I seem to have a method which many people have used to produce the children they want. As long as you have a steady, balanced approach to this whole subject and are fully prepared to love and welcome whatever baby arrives there can be no harm in trying a little 'management' to conceive the sex which would be — in the words of so many of the families who tried — the icing on the cake.

LET US KNOW YOUR RESULTS

We'd love to hear from readers who try Hazel's method. We've listed some questions we'd specially like to know the answers to, but do tell us anything else you think relevant — whatever the outcome!

Do you already have children, and if so what sex are they?

Why did you specially want a girl or a boy?

How did you pinpoint ovulation, and how easy did you find this?

Can you be sure you know when your baby was conceived?

Did you try any other methods as well as Hazel's?

Did you get the boy or girl you hoped for, and if so can you say what difference it has made to your family?

If you did not conceive the sex you hoped for, how do you feel?

Write to: Hazel Phillips, 42 Flower Lane, Mill Hill, London NW7 2JL. (Your replies will be treated in strictest confidence.)

BIBLIOGRAPHY

Hazel Phillips, *Girl or Boy? I Chose my Child* (1980).

Margaret Wynn and Arthur Wynn, *Prevention of Handicap and the Health of Women* (Routledge and Kegan Paul, 1979).

The Prevention of Handicap of Early Pregnancy Origin (Foundation for Education and Research in Childbearing, 1981).

Tessa Hilton, 'Get Set For Conception', *Mother and Baby* (June, 1982).

——, 'New Findings on Male Infertility', *Mother and Baby* (August, 1981).

Proposals for Nutritional Guidelines for Health Education in Britain prepared for the National Advisory Committee on Nutrition Education (NACNE) (Health Education Council, September, 1983).

Pregnancy Book (Health Education Council, 1984).

Getting Fit for Pregnancy (Maternity Alliance, July, 1982).

Barbara Pickard, *Are You Fit Enough to Become Pregnant?* (University of Leeds, 1983).

Guidelines for Future Parents (Foresight, 1981).

Dr Alan Maryon-Davis with Jane Thomas, *Diet 2000* (Pan, 1984).

Roy Levin, 'Current Sex Pre-Selection Methods', *International Planned Parenthood Medical Bulletin*, Vol. 16, No. 1 (February, 1982).

Ward Rinehart, *Population Reports*, Series 1, No. 2, (The George

Washington University Medical Centre, May, 1975).

Geraldine Lux Flanagan, *The First Nine Months of Life* (Heinemann, 1962).

Derek Llewellyn-Jones, *Fundamentals of Obstetrics and Gynaecology*, Volume 1 (Faber and Faber, 1969).

Frances E. Kobrin and Robert G. Potter, 'Sex Selection Through Amniocentesis and Selective Abortion', *Sex Selection of Children* (edited by Neil G. Bennett, Academic Press, 1983).

Alan S. Parkes, *Sexuality and Reproduction* (Perspectives in Biology and Medicine, 1974).

John A. Pollard, *Gender Selection. Science and Public Policy* (February, 1982).

N. E. Williamson et. al., 'Evaluation of an Unsuccessful Sex Preselection Clinic in Singapore', *Journal of Biosocial Science*, Volume 10, No. 4 (October, 1978).

Tessa Hilton, 'Boy or Girl — Take Your Pick?' *Mother and Baby* (June, 1979).

Anon. 'Child Sex Choice Remains Elusive', *Doctor* (May, 1981).

Anon. 'Tampering with the Unborn — Birth Pangs of a New Science', *The Economist* (14 July, 1984).

J. M. Sampson et. al., 'Shifts in Gender with AID', *Fertility and Sterility*, Volume 40, No. 4 (October, 1983).

O. L. Lloyd et. al., 'Unusual Sex Ratio of Births in an Industrial Town with Mortality Problems', *British Journal of Obstetrics and Gynaecology*, Volume 91 (September, 1984).

William M. James, 'Timing of Fertilization and the Sex Ratio of Offspring', *Sex Selection of Children* (edited by Neil G. Bennett, Academic Press, 1983).

Landrum B. Shettles and D. Rorvik, *Your Baby's Sex. Now You Can Choose* (Bantam Books, 1980).

Robert M. Glass and Ronald J. Ericsson, *Getting Pregnant in the 1980s* (University of California Press, 1982).

François Papa and Françoise Labro, *Boy or Girl? Choosing Your Child Through Diet* (Souvenir Press, 1984).

Tessa Hilton, 'Boy or Girl? How to Choose', *Woman* (25 February, 1984).

BIBLIOGRAPHY

P. Weideger, *Female Cycles* (Woman's Press Ltd., 1982).

Katia and Jonathan Drake, *Natural Birth Control* (Thorsons, 1984).

Zandria Pauncefort, *Choices in Contraception* (Pan, 1984).

Family Planning Using the Safe Period (Family Planning Association leaflet, 1984).

Tessa Hilton, 'Boy or Girl?' *Mother and Baby* (November, 1980).

Tessa Hilton, 'Baby Sex Choice' *Mother and Baby* (November, 1982).

Report of the Committee of Inquiry into Human Fertilization and Embryology (Command Paper 9314. 18 July, 1984).

Handbook of Medical Ethics (British Medical Association, 1984).

John C. Fletcher, 'Ethics and Public Policy: Should Sex Choice be Discouraged?' *Sex Selection of Children* (Academic Press, 1983).

Nancy E. Williamson, 'Parental Sex Preferences and Sex Selection', *Sex Selection of Children* (Academic Press, 1983).

Tabitha M. Powledge, 'Toward a Moral Policy for Sex Choice', *Sex Selection of Children* (Academic Press, 1983).

Caroline Smith and Barbara Lloyd, *Maternal Behaviour and Perceived Sex of Infant* (Child Development, 1978).

Tessa Hilton, 'Pink for a Girl . . .', *Mother and Baby* (December, 1980).

Sara Stein, *Girls and Boys* (Chatto and Windus, 1984).

Judith Arcana, *Every Mother's Son* (The Women's Press, 1983).

Elena Gianni Belotti, *Little Girls* (Writers and Readers Publishing Co-operative, 1975).

I. K. Barthaker, *The Predetermination of Sex* (Shillong, India, 1976).

INDEX